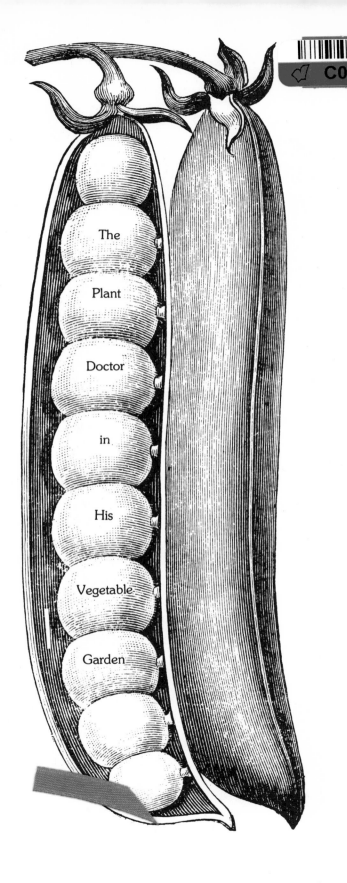

The

Plant

Doctor

in

His

Vegetable

Garden

C0-CEK-909

THE PLANT DOCTOR IN HIS VEGETABLE GARDEN

BY RICHARD NICHOLLS

Edited by Frank Wilson

Copyright © 1976 Running Press
All rights reserved under the Pan-American and International Copyright Convention

Printed in the United States of America

Distributed in Canada by Van Nostrand Reinhold Ltd., Ontario

Library of Congress Catalog Card Number 75-46631

ISBN 0 914294 45 8 Trade paperback
ISBN 0 914294 46 8 Library edition

Art Direction by Jim Wilson
Cover Illustration by Peter Ruge
Interior Design and Layout by Tom Fetterman
Interior Illustration by Elaine Brody

Library of Congress Cataloging in Publication Data

Nicholls, Richard, 1949-
   The plant doctor in his vegetable garden.

   Bibliography: p.
   Includes index.
   1. Vegetable gardening.   I.   Title.
SB321.N48   635   75-46631
ISBN 0-914294-46-8 lib. bdg.
ISBN 0-914294-45-8 pbk.

This book may be ordered directly from the publisher. Please include 25¢ postage.

Try your bookstore first.

Running Press, 38 South Nineteenth Street, Philadelphia, Pennsylvania
19103

CONTENTS

FIRST WORDS

There are no mysteries to successful vegetable gardening. There are steps that must be followed in planning and preparing the garden, and a series of procedures to be regularly repeated after the seeds have been tucked into the ground. If problems occur, there are a number of simple, effective remedies which you can select and apply. But there are no secrets.

When I planted my first vegetable garden, I didn't think things were that clear cut. I assumed that my neighbors' gardens produced such large yields because of some formula that they had mastered and I hadn't. I neglected some of the basics of good gardening in my attempt to uncover the "secrets" of getting things to grow. Failure is a forceful educator. My garden produced uninspiring results because I'd been too busy trying new fertilizers, mulching, trenching and fiddling about to carry out the basics of garden care.

That winter I picked up several books on vegetable gardening. The following spring I drew up a methodical plan for my gardening. I read about and practiced the procedures of gardening again and again until I was satisfied that I thoroughly understood them. That summer, I followed my plan from step to step, and from procedure to procedure. Where my feverish experimentation had failed, my plan succeeded. I had the kind of garden I'd admired in my neighbors' yards. Good gardening is the methodical application of basic principles and common sense.

This book was inspired, in a sense, by my mistakes. It is my hope that it will serve to prevent you from making the mistakes I made, and to guide you into the practices of good gardening that bring success and satisfaction. Now no one can entirely avoid making mistakes. But only the big mistakes are disruptive.

The very worst mistake a first-time gardener can make, in my opinion, is to start growing vegetables on a large scale. I suggest that you begin vegetable gardening in a small patch. Use your first summer to master the basics, to get the feel of your tools and become familiar with the needs of your crops. Enlarge your garden your second summer. For while a large garden can yield a heavy harvest, it can also cause a beginner frustration and disappointment. A large garden will require more time and more effort than a small plot. If there is a serious infestation of pests, or if some of the crops become diseased, the garden may be devastated before you can settle on the proper course of action. In my opinion, and based on my experience, the first rule of vegetable gardening is "Don't take on more than you can handle!"

My own experiences figure heavily in the book. But I've also learned many things of immediate, practical value from fellow gardeners, and most of what they've taught me has found its way into the book. Because I have a practical and rather limited background in horticulture, I have also relied heavily on information gathered from a variety of publications. This book is intended as a "first book" of vegetable gardening. I urge you not to let it be your last, for there are many excellent books on the subject. While I found many books to be clear and very useful, I didn't feel that any of the books were intended primarily for beginners. None of them answered all of the questions that I had. Some of the books assumed a level of sophistication on the subject that I entirely lacked. However, after I had gotten the basics down, I found the majority of books on the subject to be both helpful and entertaining.

The information in this book is arranged in the order that you should require it. Before you can begin planting, you need a good location for your garden, and a plan to guide you in sowing the crops. The soil must be turned and, if it is found lacking in some nutrient, it must be treated with manure, fertilizer or compost. After the seeds or seedlings have been planted, they must be given proper care, and they must receive water and fertilizer as they need it. A chapter on pests and diseases explains the causes, symptoms and remedies for a variety of common problems. A final chapter covers the procedures for harvesting the crops, and suggests some methods for handling them after they have been removed from the garden. A survey of the basics of vegetable gardening must necessarily be rather general. Profiles of twenty of the most popular vegetables supply specific information on the needs of each crop.

Any book on the procedures and the mechanics of gardening runs the risk of entirely losing the spirit of the endeavor. Gardening is not a mechanical pasttime. However, if you fail to master the basics of gardening, you may never get so far as to discover its very individual pleasures. Such pleasures exist to be discovered over and over again by each gardener, when his crops first push above the surface, as they rapidly develop, and when the vegetables, large, colorful, home-grown, are brought at last to the table.

Chapter  One

TOOLS

You need only a few tools to tend a small vegetable garden, and those few are moderately priced and easy to handle. Tending a large garden doesn't require more tools, just more expensive ones, since in that case, to save time and to spare yourself some hard work, you should buy either a rotary tiller or a tractor.

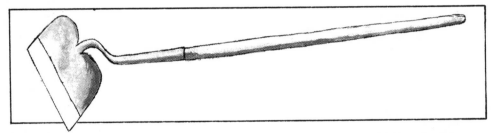

The most basic gardening implement is the hoe, which is used to break up encrusted soil, to remove weeds, and to pull soil over seeds. Different kinds of hoes, each with differently shaped blades, are available. The Reisch hoe, for instance, has a narrow pointed blade, which makes it ideal for cultivating between plants. The most versitile hoe, in my opinion, is the square-bladed hoe. But whatever kind you choose, select a light hoe, for you will be wielding it frequently, and for lengthy periods.

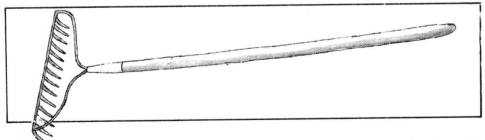

The bow rake looks like an oversized comb fastened to a long handle. A sturdy tool, it can be used to clear ground of rocks, pieces of wood, clumps of soil, and other debris. It is ideal for spreading and removing mulches. Of the several different kinds of rakes, I have found this the most useful in a vegetable garden.

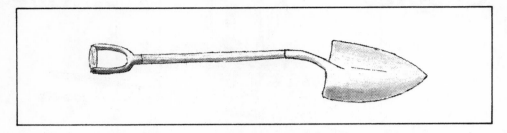

In a garden, a good shovel is indispensible. You need it for digging trenches, for scooping up and applying materials, for edging, and even for cultivating. The garden shovel is lighter and smaller than other shovels; that makes it well suited for use in your vegetable patch. But if you find yourself faced with an expanse of hardened ground to break and turn, a long handled shovel will give you better leverage — and so put less strain on your back.

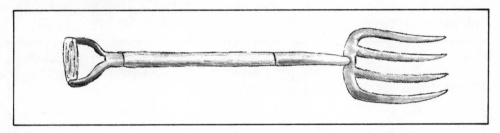

A spading fork is essential for breaking and turning the soil. It can also be used to pick up and distribute mulches, to carry away dead foliage, and to turn the layers of compost in your compost pile. The fork's tines should be of steel, which is less likely to bend. Its wooden handle should be long, so as to spare your back and provide additional leverage.

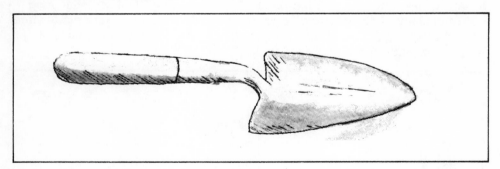

The trowel is the most versatile of tools. It is needed for all kinds of close work that cannot safely be done using a full-sized tool. During the spring especially, scarcely a day will go by when you won't find yourself using your trowel for something or other. For that reason, you should shop around until you find one that feels light and well-balanced.

A wheelbarrow or garden cart will prove quite handy in moving loads of soil, cuttings, mulches, compost, or harvested vegetables about the garden. A steel barrow is noticeably heavier than its aluminum counterpart, but is also much less likely to be bent out of shape by a heavy load. Several large garden carts are now available. Their manufacturers claim that, because they are less likely to tip over, require less energy to move, and can carry larger loads, they are better than wheelbarrows. The carts have wooden sides, an open back, and two sturdy tires.

In a large garden, power equipment is bound to save you a lot of work. A rotary tiller, or a small tractor, can, in less than a day, break and turn the soil in a sizable plot. Working in the sun with a hoe, shovel, and rake, the same job might take you a week. Machines can be used for a number of other jobs in your garden, when they are coupled with a variety of attachments. Their greatest drawback is their cost. Both start at about four hundred dollars, and many models cost as much as a thousand — not counting accessories. If you do need a tiller or tractor, explore first the possibility either of renting one, or of hiring someone who has one to do the job for you. Frankly, unless you are very serious about gardening, such a large outlay of cash is unwise. It would be better, at least at the start, to keep the size of your garden within manageable dimensions. Perhaps you could collect several gardening friends who would be willing to share the cost of a machine. Sharing will bring a tiller within your budget, but you will have to deal with the problems that occur when anything is cooperatively owned. If you decide to buy a machine, shop carefully, and compare a number of models. (A list of tiller and tractor manufacturers can be found in the appendix.)

When you purchase tools, buy quality, not quantity. Throughout the spring and summer you'll be using the basic tools again and again. Cheap tools do not do as good a job, do not last as long, and will probably give you blisters. Your tools should all have oak handles. Oak holds up longer than other woods, and is less likely to bend, splinter, or break. Metal parts should be forged of heavy gauge steel, which will outlast an alloy, stay sharp, and not bend.

Get the lightest tools you can. You'll be using them frequently, and extra weight on a tool can tire you out. However, remember that a heavier tool will probably last longer and do a better job.

You can greatly extend the life of your tools by taking proper care of them. Keep them free of dirt or dust. In the fall, clean them with warm water and a stiff wire brush. Clots of soil left on a steel part for more than a week or two will cause the part to rust. If a handle develops splinters, use a sheet of medium sandpaper to smooth it.

Rinse your wheelbarrow or cart after use, or at least once a week. Before storing it for the winter, oil the movable parts.

Keep your cutting tools sharp. You can sharpen the hoe yourself, by drawing a file across the blade in one direction. Other blunted tools may have to be sharpened by someone with special equipment and experience.

Keep your tools in order. Don't let them lay about — they'll soon disappear, or start to rust. Securely suspend sharp tools in an out-of-the-way spot, high enough so that children cannot reach them. Try to keep all of your tools in one spot, whether it be a tool shed or a portion of your cellar or utility room.

In the fall, coat all metal parts with a light dressing of oil or cup grease. A container of oiled sand will be doubly useful. Thrust the tools into the sand after using them. Sand is abrasive enough to scour away dirt, and the oil will coat the tools and protect them from rust between use or throughout the winter.

Take care of your tools, and they'll last a long time and give you good service.

Chapter  Two

PLANNING

Selecting a Location

Before you turn that first spadeful of soil in your garden, there are several preliminary steps you must take. The first is to select a location for your vegetable patch; the amount of acceptable land available, and its shape, will largely determine the size and arrangement of your garden. Then, you have to decide which vegetables you want to grow, and in what quantities. Finally, you should draw to scale a plan for your garden, indicating therein the location of each crop.

What qualities indicate a favorable location?

Sunlight. This is the single most important factor to consider. Your garden must receive at least 6 hours of sunlight a day. Check a potential location several times during the day, in order to be certain that the shadows of trees or buildings do not darken it for any length of time. Try to locate your garden at least two feet away from any tree: not only will the tree stand between your vegetables and the sun, but its roots will compete with those of your vegetables for nutrients and moisture. In such a competition, your garden is bound to lose. The best location for your garden is any piece of ground clear of obstacles and untroubled by shadows.

Good water drainage. Continuously waterlogged ground can damage plants by acting as a medium for the growth and spread of destructive molds and funguses. If at all possible, avoid low-lying ground, or ground that retains large puddles, or that is regularly flooded. If you have no alternative, however, you can, at some extra effort and expense, salvage such ground by improving the soil and installing drains.

Good air drainage. A plot of ground higher than the surrounding terrain will receive, not only more direct sunlight, but also warmer air. A plot located in a depression, or at the base of a hill, will be slightly cooler than a higher location, because warm air rises while colder, heavier air constantly descends. Stagnant air, cold air, or early frosts can damage crops — and ground at the base of a hill or in a depression may suffer from all three.

A piece of ground having a slight slope makes an excellent location for a garden. An inclination of several degrees towards the south or west will expose the ground more directly to the sun's rays. Thus your garden will warm up earlier in the year than a level piece of ground, and will receive slightly more light throughout the summer. In addition, the slight pitch should give your garden excellent drainage. Should the location have a grade greater than ten-percent, however, you may be troubled by erosion after every heavy rain.

A gentle slope, therefore, is an excellent location for a garden, so long as it is located on the south or southwestern side of the incline. It offers ample sunlight and good air and water drainage — with the bonus that a slope will protect your garden from the strong breezes that can sweep a hilltop or other level piece of ground. There is, however, one other fact that you should consider. The steeper a slope, the thinner the soil, generally. In short, a slight inclination makes an excellent garden site, but a steep hillside does not.

Good gardening soil is often indicated by a healthy crop of weeds or grass. One farmer told me that, when he shops for farming land, he looks for a good, thick crop of weeds. For if a piece of ground can support weeds, grasses, or wildflowers, it will certainly produce large, healthy vegetables. If you are uncertain of the quality of your soil, consider having it tested by the agricultural service. Soil suitable for supporting crops should be able to accept water without becoming clotted and waterlogged. It should be loose enough to be workable. It should have a store of organic materials (making it dark and moist to the touch). Soil is, however, one of the most malleable elements in your garden. There are many steps you can take to improve its drainage and nutrient content. Even the most unpromising soil can be treated to produce large, healthy crops of vegetables. (For additional information on soil, see Chapter 5).

If strong winds occasionally blow across your property, you will have to erect a windbreak to protect your crops. If you are pressed for space, a windbreak of clear fiberglass will admit light to your garden while shielding it from winds. A hedge or a fence standing in the path of the prevailing wind will also make a serviceable windbreak, so long as either is located too far from the garden to cast shadows on the plants. If you have a choice of locations, select that piece least troubled by wind.

There is no reason to surrender convenience in the selection of a location. Plant your garden as close to your house as you can without short-changing your plants. However, you should not plant within two feet of the house: you will have trouble with shadows, and may have trouble with the soil. Lime, leached away from the cement foundation of a house, can accumulate in sufficient quantities in the soil around a house to damage vegetable plants.

To avoid a summer-long struggle with lengths of hose, keep in mind the location of your outdoor water faucet when you are choosing a plot. Remember — the first and most important requirement for your garden is sunlight. If a piece of ground is well-drained, sheltered from the wind, but receives ample air circulation, is close to your house, but is in partial or complete shade, it is largely useless as a vegetable garden. Some crops will adapt to partial shade, but most will not. They will languish and die.

Few gardeners are so fortunate as to have a plot answering all of these requirements. But only sunlight is vital. Steps can be taken to remedy other problems, but sunlight is either present or it isn't. A plot suffering from bad drainage can be drained, and its soil improved. If you must garden in a depression, you can use a coldframe or a hotbed to protect the tenderest crops, and can adjust your growing schedule to take into account the chance of late spring or early fall frosts.

What if you have several small pieces of ground that fulfill most of the requirements, but no single piece of substantial size? Garden on each of them. It may mean extra work for you, and some inconvenience, but if that is the best your property offers, do it! The most important quality a gardener can have is the ability to adapt to existing conditions and put them to advantage. So if you can't have one large garden, have several vestpocket plots. Save the sunny locations for vegetables, and plant more adaptable flowers in the shady parts of your property. Utilizing all of the available space will allow you to grow substantial numbers of vegetables.

The Size of Your Garden

But how many vegetables do you want? How much do you think you can handle? My own experience, and the experience of other gardeners I have spoken to, indicates that most first-time gardeners plant too much. What seemed like a great idea in April becomes an exhausting reality by July. So start modestly.

To supply a family of four with vegetables throughout most of the year, you will need a plot at least 50' long by 25' wide. Keeping a family of six self-sufficient in vegetables will require a garden 100' by 50'. Many first-time gardeners have of course tended large plots successfully. But a large garden does take more time, and more energy, than a modest one. Moreover, beginning gardeners are obviously more prone to make mistakes than experienced gardeners — and are generally less able to correct them.

Use your first year of vegetable gardening to "get the hang of it" — to master the tools and techniques of gardening, to become familiar with the appearance and needs of your crops at each stage of their development, and to learn to recognize and deal with problems. Remember: it is easier to deal with an insect attack or an infection in a small garden rather than in a large one — and it's less painful to accept some losses in a small first-year garden than to lose considerable amounts from a large patch (because you didn't know what to do at the first sign of trouble). Let your first summer be a learning experience — by mastering the basics of gardening now, you'll avoid problems later on. In addition, if your soil is depleted and requires additional nutrients and soil components, you can work on improving it during your first summer of gardening. By the time you are ready for your second year of planting, your once-exhausted soil should be in excellent shape.

It is also worth considering how great a yield you can harvest from a small vegetable patch. A garden 15' long and 10' wide will yield a considerable amount of variety of vegetables. A 25' by 20' patch should give a family of four or six more vegetables than they can immediately consume, and so provide a surplus for canning or storage for later use.

Don't let the question of size confuse you. A small plot, well tended, will produce more than you expect, and possibly more than you can consume. A small garden will allow you to familiarize yourself with gardening procedures, and will give you an opportunity to devote additional time to the improvement of your soil.

If you have settled on planting a large garden, go ahead. But do try to recruit some help. One person can easily prepare and maintain a small garden, but tending a large garden can be a formidable task. No matter how large or small your garden, turning it into a family project should shorten the time required to tend it, and provide an excellent activity for the entire family to participate in. A vegetable garden is also an excellent vehicle for introducing children to the world of green growing things.

Planning Your Vegetable Garden

When you begin working on your garden, you should have a detailed plan to guide you. The dimensions of the plot, the length of the rows, and the distance between rows should all be decided and sketched out beforehand. Your blueprint for the garden should include a list of the crops you intend to raise, the location of each variety, and a notation of the earliest date on which each can be planted. By working out the layout of your garden before you begin preparing the soil, you'll be able to experiment until you are satisfied that you're making the best possible use of the space available. Moreover, by following a plan, once you begin work outdoors, you can save time and avoid confusion. It's a good deal easier to consult a plan when a question arises, then to have to work out each problem and part of the work in your head. A thorough, detailed plan will greatly reduce the chances of error.

10

Use a sheet of unlined paper or graph paper for your blueprint. Draw the plan to scale (a useful scale is to have one-half inch represent a foot). Use a steel tape rule to determine the measurements of the location you've selected. Your drawing should also accurately indicate the shape of the garden. Your garden needn't be square — you can and should adapt it to the location. So long as your rows are straight and your garden well tended, it really doesn't matter if you're growing vegetables in a rectangle, a triangle, or a rhombus.

After you've drawn in the dimensions of the plot, add the rows. They should run from north to south, so that each of the crops will receive an equivalent amount of sunlight. If your garden is located on a slope, however, the rows should be laid out across the slope, regardless of whether this means from east to west: there is no other way to prevent erosion. The rows should have a width of six inches to a foot, depending on the type of crop. Root crops take up less space in a row than fruit or vine crops. The rows should be spaced three feet apart. Divide them into four or five foot segments. Each segment can be planted with a different crop. Plant long rows of a crop only if you intend to freeze or can quantities of the vegetable. Most vegetable plants produce sizable yields, and if you plant too much of a crop, you'll find yourself with more than you can immediately use.

Plants that grow very tall, such as corn and pole beans, should be planted at the northern end of the plot, so that they do not stand between other, shorter crops and the sun. Low growers, such as bush beans, broccoli, beets, cabbage, carrots, celery, cucumbers, kale, potatoes, radishes, spinach, and turnips, should be planted at the southern ends of the rows, extending towards the tall crops. Peppers, squash, and tomatoes, which reach a height about half that of the tallest crops, should be planted between short and tall vegetables. In this manner, all of the crops will receive the sunlight they need. If the tall crops cannot be located along the northern end of the plot, place them next to a crop that can adapt to partial shade, such as cucumbers or lettuce. Or they can be planted between two fast growing crops. By the time corn has grown tall enough to block the sun, your fast crop will be ready for harvesting.

Perennial crops, such as asparagus and rhubarb, remain in the ground year after year, producing a new crop each summer. They grow rather tall, and should be located at the northern end of the plot. Plant them in a spot where they can remain undisturbed, without complicating your work in the garden. A corner location is preferable.

Several other factors must be taken into consideration when you begin selecting crops and arranging them in your plan. You must determine how many days each crop requires to reach maturity, and how early or late in the season it can be planted.

Succession planting means staggering your crops. Some crops, commonly described as "cool season" vegetables, can be planted early in the spring, harvested by midsummer, and planted again for harvesting in the fall. Such crops don't do their best in very warm weather. "Warm season" crops, on the other hand, cannot be planted until all danger of frost has passed, and the soil has been warmed by the sun. They can be damaged by cool weather, and should be planted so that they mature before the onset of fall. Broccoli, carrots, celery, onions, peas, potatoes, radishes, spinach, and turnips are all cool season crops. Warm season crops include beans, corn, cucumbers, eggplants, onion, peppers, and tomatoes.

You can greatly increase the yield of your garden by planting several cool season crops as early as you can in the spring. As soon as they have matured and been harvested, pull the plants out, turn the soil, give it a dose of fertilizer or compost, and sow a warm season crop in the same place. After you have harvested the warm season crop, you may still have time to plant a cool crop for harvest in the fall. Typical successions include: radishes or spinach, to bush beans or cabbage, lettuce or eggplant, or early peas to corn. Never follow a root crop with a root crop, or a fruit crop with a fruit crop. Within families, vegetables share the need for certain nutrients. For instance, leaf crops consume a lot of nitrogen. If you follow a cool season leaf crop with a warm season leaf crop, the warm crop will need the now-depleted nitrogen. You can avoid this by treating each piece of ground with a dose of fertilizer and organic materials, after the first crop has been harvested and before the second goes in. If a crop has been attacked by insects, they may remain in the ground after the crop has been harvested. Frequently, insects attracted to a crop find other, similar crops equally attractive — but they may be repelled by a crop of another family. So plan for succession plantings. And rotate the crops, so that members of the same family do not follow one another in a row.

Plant a crop at several intervals, so that you have a constant supply of vegetables, but not too many. You can, for example, plant a five foot row of lettuce a third at a time, in three weekly intervals. Or you can plant several short rows, spacing each several days to a week apart. As each row matures, it can be harvested, cleared, and replanted. Either way, you'll have a steady supply of the crop, but won't be burdened with more of a perishable vegetable than you can immediately use. Unless you take steps to avoid it, too large a harvest, maturing within a few days, can be as troublesome as a harvest that falls short of your expectations.

Information on planting dates and the length of growing seasons can be found in seed catalogs and in the Profiles section of this book. Your county agricultural agent will be able to answer any specific questions regarding planting dates for your area. Different varieties of the same crop require differing amounts of time to mature, so research the subject carefully.

15 × 12 Garden

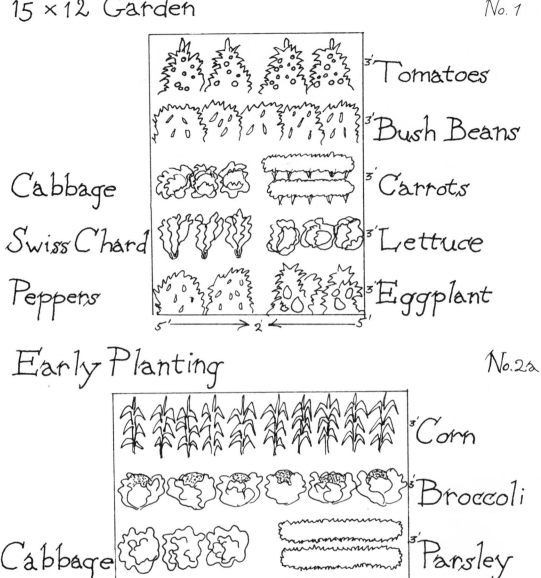

Tomatoes — 3'

Bush Beans — 3'

Cabbage | Carrots — 3'

Swiss Chard | Lettuce — 3'

Peppers | Eggplant — 3'

5' ← → 2' ← → 5'

Early Planting

Corn — 3'

Broccoli — 3'

Cabbage | Parsley — 3'

Celery | Turnips — 3'

Onion Sets | Carrots — 3'

Spinach | Lettuce — 3'

6½' ← → ↑ ← → 6½'

15' × 20'

Space 1½' between crops

Midsummer, Late Summer Plantings

15'x20'   S

Broccoli
or
Brussels Sprouts

Peas

Beets

Parsnips

Carrots

Lettuce

Spinach

Potatoes

Kale

Summer
Squash

N

Cucumbers or bush beans or peas
on trellis

Can be added in late spring, early summer

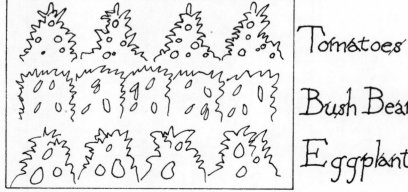

Tomatoes

Bush Beans

Eggplant

14

There is one other factor that you may want to take into consideration when planning the layout of your garden. Certain plants appear to benefit from being planted next to a specific crop. For instance, asparagus and tomato plants seem to be of mutual benefit to each other, as do carrots and peas, cabbages and tomatoes, celery and beans, and turnips and peas. Radishes seem to do well with any vegetable. Some of these combinations are successful because the plants have different needs and don't compete for nutrients. Others succeed because they do not battle for light. Some plants actually serve to repel pests from their neighbors, and so form a mutual defense association. All of the reasons why these combinations seem to work are not clear, but work they do.

Intercropping — mixing crops together — helps make the best use of all available space. Mix the seeds of a quick growing crop in with the seeds of a slow-to-mature crop, or plant a row of a fast crop between two rows of slow crops. Lettuce, a fast crop, can be mixed with broccoli, cabbage or beans — all slow crops. Spinach can be planted between squash plants, or next to rows of slow-growing beans or peas. Radishes are rarely planted in a row of their own; they grow so rapidly that they are used to indicate the presence of slow-to-appear vegetables. Radishes can be mixed into a row of any crop. Intercropping will give you a more varied yield and, because the principle makes for a thorough use of space, it may give you a larger yield as well.

A detailed plan will make your work in the garden easier. Because every step and procedure will have been taken into account, you should encounter few surprises when you begin preparing the soil for crops. Your work should go faster, because you'll know exactly what to do, and in what order to do it. A good plan is one of the most important steps towards creating a healthy, productive garden.

Shopping for Seeds

You may have selected an excellent location for your garden: the soil may be dark and rich, the ground may have a slight slope and good drainage, and the spot may receive abundant sunlight. But if you sow the wrong varieties of seeds, or use seed of an inferior grade, neither the sun nor the soil can save your crops. The plants may well grow in weak or stunted. Some vegetable crops may not even survive to maturity. Selecting the right varieties of seeds for your garden is one of the most important, and most frequently overlooked, steps towards preparing a productive garden.

As soon as you select a site for your garden, get in touch with your county agricultural agent or state agricultural extension service (see Services in the appendix for further information on agricultural agents). Ask for any information they have on recommended seed varieties for your state. Extensive tests have been carried out in each state or region of the country to determine which seed varieties are best suited to the climate of the area. For instance, according to the list furnished me by my county agent, there are four varieties of lettuce seeds, and three varieties of peas that consistently produce larger, healthier crops in my state than other varieties. Fifteen varieties of tomatoes, including "Ramapo," "Big Boy Hybrid," "Manapal," "Setmore," and "Sunray," have been found to be well suited for growing in the type of climate prevalent in my home state.

Only after you have received this information should you start shopping for seeds. You'll find a list of seed supply companies doing business through the mail in the Appendix of this book. Write requesting copies of catalogs from several of the companies. While you're waiting for the catalogs to arrive, draw up a tentative list of the vegetables you intend to raise. Because of the ever-increasing number of home gardeners, it's a good idea to write for catalogs early in the spring. Several companies I wrote to in late April had already exhausted their supply. Other companies had sold out their entire stock of several seed varieties.

The garden supply centers in your area stock seeds. They are likely to have many of the brand name varieties mentioned in the literature issued by your county agent. For that reason, I make most of my seed purchases locally. When you buy locally, you can start sowing seeds, indoors or out, immediately. But seed company catalogs usually offer you a wider variety of seeds, including many hybrids and unusual varieties. Each year, for the purpose of experimentation, I order several varieties of seeds through the mail.

Even if I wasn't on the look-out for new seed varieties and ideas, I would still look forward to receiving catalogs in the mail. Many companies produce large, colorful booklets, featuring informative growing and harvesting tips. It may be some indication of my interest in gardening that I can spend a perfectly contented evening reading seed catalogs! Many of the companies also offer tools, fertilizers and gardening aids that are frequently not available in garden supply centers.

Seed catalogs are not only entertaining and informative; they are also, quite often, confusing. The problem occurs because seedsmen are in a very competitive business: when you take that into account, it may seem less perplexing to discover that each company claims its varieties are the best, and produce the largest, juiciest, and most attractive crops.

If you remember to shop from the list provided by your state agricultural service, you can avoid most of the confusion such conflicting claims can cause. And if you are interested in varieties not mentioned on your list, you should be able to select an acceptable variety by keeping several points in mind.

Purchase only those varieties described in specific terms. Be suspicious of very general descriptions, or claims for "magical results." Look for information on the estimated number of days required for a crop to reach maturity. But remember that such estimates are based on ideal conditions. The climate of your area, as well as the mildness or harshness of the weather during the spring and summer, can add and — more rarely — subtract days from that estimate.

The most reliable catalogs include information on the unusual qualities of a variety, its flavor, and its uses. Some varieties must be used as they are harvested. Others are especially good canned or frozen. The seeds of some vegetables vulnerable to a specific disease are now frequently treated to be resistant to that infection. Some catalogs include an estimate of how many plants, or how long a row, can be produced from a packet of seeds. Specific information on starting, tending and harvesting a crop is also quite helpful, and is an indication of the interest a supplier has in his customers.

In short, you can generally tell how good a catalog is, and by extension the quality of its products, by the amount of information given, and by the degree to which it is specific and clear.

The packets of seeds you receive in the mail, or purchase at a garden supply center, will include information on how to plant them, and on any unusual qualities the seeds possess. In addition, the packets will have a date stamped on them, generally including the month, always including the year. Buy only those seeds with the current year stamped on the packet. Because many seeds do not remain fresh very long, buy only as many seeds as you need.

Be a selective shopper. Check the racks of the garden centers in your area. Consult several catalogs. But always let your purchases be guided by the list furnished by your agricultural agent. Be wary of very inexpensive seeds, or seeds given free in some promotion. I once received several packets of seeds given as a bonus to anyone purchasing another item. I planted the seeds, and the few weak, stunted plants that appeared made me regret not having tossed the packets away. Buying seeds is the most important early step towards a successful, productive garden. By selecting the varieties best suited to your area, you take a very large step towards assuring yourself of a bountiful harvest.

Shopping for Seedlings

Most vegetable crops can be started easily and quickly from seed. Some crops, however, are extremely vulnerable to cool temperatures and frost, and cannot be planted until all danger of frost has passed and the days have become decidedly warm. Still, some crops, if they are to reach maturity before fall, must be planted rather early. You can get round this problem by starting such tender crops indoors, or in a coldframe or greenhouse, or you can purchase seedlings from a garden center or large grower. You will have to do the latter if you don't have the time or energy to start plants yourself.

Seedlings of some vegetables are sold in peat pots, which greatly simplify the transplanting process. The plant, still in the pot, is placed in a hole, and soil is poured around and over the pot until it is completely covered. The pot will decompose, adding some nutrients to the soil. The plant will push its roots right through the pot's walls. Keep the pot moist until it is planted; if it dries out, it will become hard and water repellent, and make it difficult for the roots to emerge.

Plants are generally available in a variety of sizes. The size of the plants you select depends entirely on your budget — smaller plants, being younger, will require more time to mature than larger plants, but should be just as healthy. Moreover, several small plants often cost little more than one large plant.

When you're shopping for seedlings, look for plants that are compact, with several sets of leaves. Avoid plants that are mostly stem, and have few leaves; their tops may have developed at the expense of the root system. Yellow or blotched leaves indicate either an infection, or inadequate nourishment. Avoid such plants. Buy only healthy seedlings — you have too much to do in your garden to spare time for nursing sickly seedlings.

When you get your purchases home, water them, and set them in spot that is sunny, but protected from the wind. A porch, a very sunny room or a coldframe are excellent temporary locations for plants. At night, cover the plants with a cardboard box — unless you are keeping them in a heated room. Expose the plants to the outdoors for gradually lengthening periods over several days. By allowing them to adapt to conditions outdoors, you avoid trauma when the plants are finally set in the ground. And while you are "hardening-off" the plants, toughening them up for life outdoors, you can be working on the soil, preparing it to receive and nourish the crops.

Coldframes and Hotbeds

Starting plants in late winter or early spring gives you a considerable head start on the usual growing season. This is especially important for crops that would otherwise require the entire summer to mature. By getting them well under way so early in the year, you should be able to fit in two plantings of the crop. If you have a sufficient amount of space and light in your home, you can start the plants indoors. If you don't have the room to start the plants in your house, you can do it outdoors, in the protected environment of a coldframe. A coldframe is a low rectangular structure, having four wooden walls, a glass or plastic top, and no bottom, as it is designed to be sunk slightly into the ground. It shields plants from the harsh weather of late winter and the uncertain weather of early spring, while admitting the sunlight so essential to the seedlings development.

It doesn't take much time, money or skill to build a coldframe. You can use discarded storm windows for the top, or a sheet of plastic or plexiglass. If you do use windows, simply take their measurements and build a box to accommodate them. The side walls should slant forward. The back wall should be two feet high, the front wall a foot high, to maximize the amount of light entering the unit. Place the coldframe so that it faces south. Once you've selected a location, mark out the measurements of the unit in the soil, and excavate the ground within the markings to a depth of eighteen inches. Treat the soil within the unit as you would if you were preparing the garden for spring planting. Shovel a foot of the soil back in after it has been treated, then set the unit in place. Detailed plans for coldframe construction can be obtained from your agricultural agent or state extension service. Prefabricated coldframes are now offered by several mail order garden supply firms.

You can sow seeds in the soil covered by the unit, or you can plant seeds in flats, and keep the flats in the coldframe until the ground has warmed sufficiently to permit transplanting seedlings into the garden. Whether you're using windows or a sheet of plastic as a cover, it will have to be firmly in place, but capable of being lifted to allow fresh air to enter the unit. Windows can be propped up, and a sheet of plastic rolled back, when ventilation is necessary. The seedlings will require the same close care you would give them if they were being raised in your house, or in the garden.

After the spring crop of seedlings have been transplanted into the garden, you can use the unit to start crops of fall vegetables, such as broccoli or cabbage. Long after the first fall frost, you can be raising fresh vegetables in the unit. Or, if you need storage space, you can fill the coldframe with layers of straw and root crops, which will keep throughout the winter.

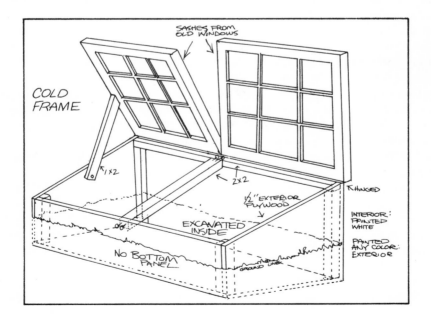

19

If you intend to grow vegetables in the unit all winter, you'll have to heat it. Inexpensive soil heating cables, which convert electricity into heat, are available from garden supply outfits and greenhouse manufacturers. The cables are buried in the soil below the unit, and maintain a steady temperature that can be set by a thermostat. Before the advent of electricity, farmers used to turn a coldframe into a hotbed by digging down to a depth of three feet within the unit, and piling in a mixture of fresh manure and straw. The mix would be two to two and a half feet deep, and would then be covered by six to eight inches of soil, in which seeds would then be sown. The fermenting mix would generate a considerable amount of warmth — enough to sustain seedlings through wintry weather.

A coldframe makes a valuable, versatile, inexpensive addition to any vegetable garden. For only a little more money, you can convert your coldframe into a hotbed.

If you don't have enough level land for a garden, adapt your plans to the shape of the land available. If the only possible location for your garden is on a slope, then make your garden there. With some extra labor, you can overcome the problems that gardening on an incline presents.

Your garden will have to be on the south side of the hill, if it is to receive adequate sunlight. Run the rows across the slope, rather than straight up and down it. Rows running from top to bottom encourage erosion. A thick layer of compost, laid along the bottom of each row, will absorb any water or soil runoff.

Creating terraces on the slope is the best, but most demanding, solution to the problem of hillside gardening. You will have to dig enough soil out of the slope to create a series of "steps" — level areas reinforced by retaining walls of wood or stone. It isn't easy work, and it should be considered only if no other alternative is open to you. If you must do it, you might find some solace in the fact that farmers in South America and the Orient have been growing crops on terraces for thousands of years. And for most of that time, they had only the most primitive of tools to excavate the hillsides. Lacking wheelbarrows, they hauled the excess soil away in baskets. And in the most unpromising sites, they created luxuriant food gardens.

Keeping Records

Keep a record of the layout of your garden, and of the dates and specifics of care for each crop. What varieties did you plant? How much of each? When? And when did you harvest the crop? Did you fertilize with chemicals or organic materials? Did you use compost? How successful was the crop? This information may be of help to you next year, when it comes time to select crops and map out another plan.

Keep a notebook handy, and record such information throughout the summer. In the fall, when you can sit down and study the record, patterns may begin to emerge, and problems you encountered may begin to make sense, when you discover that a mistake was made. Next spring, read through the notes again before you draw up your plan. Perhaps you'll want to alter planting dates, or switch to another variety of a crop, or alter your treatment of the crop. Unless you have a record to consult, you may forget such important information, and go on to make the same mistakes, all over again.

You become a better gardener by learning from your mistakes. But you can't do that, and you can't repeat your successes, unless you clearly remember them.

Chapter

Three

VEGETABLE PROFILES

Vegetables have much in common, but no two crops have exactly the same requirements for sowing or cultivation. Some can be planted as soon as the danger of frost has passed, others cannot be planted until the weather has become consistently warm. Some crops require more attention than others. The amounts of water and fertilizer vegetables need vary greatly. Because of these differences, and because you must give a crop exactly what it wants if it is to mature, this chapter consists of individual profiles of twenty of the most frequently grown vegetables. Each profile includes information on when to plant seeds or seedlings, how to plant, the proper care of a crop, common diseases and pests and their remedies, and how to harvest the crop.

Many points mentioned briefly in the profiles are discussed at length elsewhere in the text. The specifics of sowing seed, transplanting seedlings, preparing rows, and watering, weeding and feeding a crop are discussed in the following chapters. You may wish to skim through this chapter in order to get some idea of the vegetables you'd like to include in your plot — but I urge you to read the entire book before beginning your garden. Enthusiasm is a necessary quality in a gardener — but enthusiasm not allied to knowledge is certain to cause trouble.

Seed varieties are not given in the profiles, because such information could be very misleading. As mentioned previously, different varieties of a crop are required in different areas. Your county agricultural agent or state agricultural extension service can provide you with specific information on the varieties best suited to your soil and climate.

To allow quick reference, the profiles are arranged alphabetically.

Beans

Beans take up little space, can be grown in most kinds of soil, produce large crops, and are easy to cultivate. Moreover, instead of reducing the nutrients in the soil, beans serve to increase them. Their roots produce a bacterium that stores nitrogen, an element important for producing healthy plants. In fact, the roots continue to release nitrogen into the soil even after the beans are harvested.

There are many varieties of beans, but those most frequently recommended for home gardening are the "snap" beans. These are available in "bush" and "pole" forms. Bush beans are self-supporting plants that grow close to the ground. Pole beans grow upwards in long tendrils, and must be provided with a pole, a taut rope, or some other form of support. Many gardeners grow pole beans on a fence or trellis.

Bush varieties mature faster. They require little cultivation and produce a heavy yield. Pole varieties mature more slowly, and require additional care, but take up a minimum of space. They also produce larger yields over a greater period than do bush types. Some gardeners claim that pole varieties taste better than bush beans, but I have never noticed any appreciable difference.

Snap Beans

Snap beans, also known as string beans, can be grown in almost any kind of soil. Bush snap beans can be grown in an area having as few as 65-70 warm days. Pole snaps need an additional week to ten days to mature. You can plant the seeds as soon as the soil temperature reaches 65°. If you don't have a soil thermometer (an inexpensive and worthwhile addition to your gardening equipment) to check the warmth of the soil, you can go by the trees in your area. As soon as the hickories or the oaks, or any other late-leafing trees produce green leaves, the soil is warm enough to plant beans.

Bush seeds should be planted 1½ to 2 inches deep, 3 inches apart, in rows 1½ to 2 feet apart. Pole seeds should be spaced at intervals of from 9 inches to a foot, and the rows should be 2½ to 3 feet apart. When the bush plants are 2 to 3 inches high the rows should be thinned to allow 6 inches between plants. You can assure yourself of a steady supply of beans by additional plantings every two weeks until midsummer, or roughly 60 days before the projected first frost.

Bean rows have to be weeded thoroughly and regularly, and the soil should be frequently stirred. Don't dig into the soil — cultivate it lightly with a hoe: deep cultivation can damage the roots. Unless there are frequent and heavy rains, you will have to water the plants. Do this by soaking the soil — don't pour water onto the foliage: it encourages disease. A thin layer of mulch around the plants will help the soil retain moisture and prevent the surface around the plants from becoming encrusted. The plants should be fertilized every three to four weeks. Compost may be applied — lightly. Too much compost can encourage the development of foliage — and you want to raise beans, not bean leaves.

Several species of beetle and moth larvae are partial to bean plants. The best way to control a mild infestation is to check each of the leaves and pick off any bugs you find. By regularly inspecting all of your vegetables for signs of insect or disease attacks, you can reduce the seriousness and the frequency of such problems. Because many insects are nocturnal feeders, I've found it a good idea to check out the patch by flashlight once a week. You may not want to do it quite so often, but an occasional nighttime prowl can prove revealing. (See chapter 9 for information on identifying and treating plant pests and diseases).

Allowing beans to ripen on the plant causes a plant to cease producing pods and die. A plant that has been cleared of its pods before they ripen will continue to produce pods. So bean pods must be picked while still immature. The pods should be picked when they are about 3 inches long; their tips will be soft, and they should snap off of a stem easily. Hold the stem of a plant with one hand as you gently snap off the pods with your free hand. Broken stems will reduce a plant's productiveness, and may even kill it. Once the plants have stopped producing pods, pull them out and add them to your compost heap, or leave them in and till them thoroughly into the soil. A fall crop of beets or carrots can then be sown where the beans stood — they'll benefit from the nitrogen the beans have added to the soil.

Beets

Beets are one of the most practical vegetables you can grow. They do quite well in any consistency of soil, aside from a heavy clay type. Seeds and seedlings both are resistant to frost and so can be planted in early spring. Beets suffer from few pests or diseases, require a minimum of space, and return a high yield — and both leaves and bulb are edible. An excellent source of vitamins, beets are also easy to store.

Beet seeds should be planted as soon as the ground is warm enough to be cultivated. They may be planted in either single or wide rows; whichever you use, the rows should be from one to two feet apart. The seeds should be placed in holes one inch deep, and spaced one to two inches apart. If you want a steady supply of beets through summer and into fall, start with two rows and add a row at three-week intervals. But if your family isn't that fond of beets, one planting should be enough. After harvesting, you can turn the soil and plant something else. Many seed companies offer "early" and "main crop" beets. "Early" types are meant to be planted in the spring; "main crop" or late beets need warm weather for maximum growth and flavor, and should be planted either in late spring or early summer.

Each beet seed can produce two to six plants, so beets must be carefully thinned. Begin thinning when the plants are from four to five inches above the surface, and remove the smaller plants until there is at least four inches between the plants remaining. Don't throw any healthy thinnings away: the small beets are edible when you cook the entire plant — both leaves and bulbs. Because beet seedlings take time to appear, a few radish seeds sown with the beets will help you to identify the rows, and perhaps save you from confusing very young seedlings with weeds.

If there is little rain, you will have to water the rows to keep the plants from drying out. An occasional watering should be all that is required. Don't allow the soil around the plants to become hard and compacted — to keep the soil sufficiently loose, water it and break it up. A light dressing once a month of a "complete" fertilizer (see chapter 7 for fertilizers) will spur growth and keep the beets tender.

25

Other types of fertilizer can be used, but never apply fresh manure to beets: the plants can be badly burned. Well-rotted manure, however, as well as a dressing of compost, will have a positive effect on the crop.

Compost also benefits a beet crop by discouraging attacks of root maggots. These will tunnel into the roots or leaves of a plant, damaging and even killing it. By applying a heavy dressing of compost, and by changing the site of your beet rows each year, you can avoid any severe infestation. Slugs may begin feeding on the leaves of the beet. They are most active in the evening and at night, and are quite noticeable. Remove any you discover.

Broccoli

Broccoli is a hardy, cool season plant; it is particularly rich in vitamins A, B, C, calcium, and iron. A member of the cabbage family, it prefers cool weather; so it's a good idea to start plants indoors about a month before the projected date of the last frost in your area. Sow the seeds in containers having a mix of sterile soil and moss, or soil and vermiculite. Cover the container with a sheet of glass or plastic to retain moisture, and lay a sheet of cardboard over the container to block out sunlight. When the seeds germinate, thin out the rows. Expose the seedlings to conditions outdoors by placing them in a coldframe or on a windowsill by an open window a week before you intend to set them out. Transplant the seedlings to the garden, spacing them at intervals of from two to two-and-a-half feet. The point of all this effort is to bring the plants to maturity before very warm weather arrives. Broccoli requires between fifty-five and sixty days to grow from seed to maturity.

Broccoli can adapt to almost any kind of soil, so long as the ground is well drained. This is especially important because the vegetable requires frequent watering, and a soil incapable of absorbing large amounts of water would soon become waterlogged and provide an excellent medium for the growth of molds and funguses. Applications of a fertilizer rich in nitrogen will encourage the rapid growth of the plants. As with many other vegetables, it's a good idea to plant several seedlings each at two or three week intervals, to insure that the entire crop does not mature within several days. Five or six plants should be sufficient to supply a family of six with all the broccoli they want.

Cultivate the ground around the plants frequently, but gently. Broccoli's roots remain quite close to the surface, and can be easily damaged.

Broccoli has a main stalk, at the top of which a cluster of small, dark green buds develops. Using a sharp knife, sever the stalk about four inches below the buds. After the central head is harvested, numbers of small lateral roots will develop and produce flower buds that are likewise edible. Harvesting shoots before they flower encourages continued production so long as the weather remains cool. Steady warmth causes the plant to flower, and to cease producing edible parts. But four to six harvests should be possible for each stalk.

Cabbage worms and aphids are both attracted to broccoli, and they can do great damage. Plants may be treated with Malathion, but only before buds form. Several diseases, including club root, black-leg and black rot, can prove fatal to broccoli. These diseases commonly attack other members of the cabbage family, so it's a good idea not to plant broccoli where cauliflower, brussels sprouts, or cabbage have previously grown.

Broccoli can also be grown as a fall crop. Sow the seed in late May or early June, after mixing a load of organic material into the spot selected for the crop. When the stalks are four inches high, thin the rows, or simply transplant some of the seedlings until there is between one-and-a-half to two feet between plants. The plants should mature after Autumn has arrived. During midsummer, if temperatures remain high for several days, it may be a good idea to protect the seedlings by shielding them from direct sunlight.

Cabbage

Cabbage is a cool weather crop and needs a regular supply of moisture. It won't do well under hot, dry conditions. You can sow crops for early summer and early fall harvesting. To be certain that spring cabbage will be mature before the weather turns very warm, begin your plants indoors. Plant the seeds in flats and give them a bright, cool location. Coldframes are an excellent place to start cabbage plants. As soon as any danger of frost has passed, set the plants in your garden. Some garden centers sell cabbage seedlings in the spring. Incidentally, when shopping for seedlings, look for a light purple shading on their leaves. This indicates that the young plants have been properly hardened off and will not go into shock when moved outdoors.

A fall crop of cabbages can be raised from seed. Sow the seeds in midsummer for a harvest in early fall. As with all other vegetables, seed packets should include an estimate of how many weeks it takes for a variety to reach maturity.

Cabbage can adapt to almost any kind of soil, but the plants require frequent light applications of fertilizer. Some gardeners dress the ground where cabbage is to be grown with a thick layer of animal manure. Spread manure over the ground in a layer two to three inches thick, then work it thoroughly into the soil. Do this two to three weeks before you intend to sow seeds or transplant seedlings.

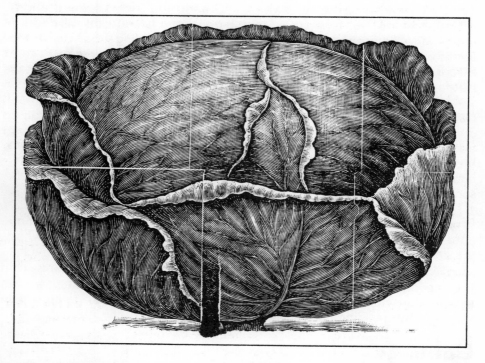

Seedlings should be planted at a distance of from fourteen to eighteen inches from one another. Rows should be two feet apart. The seedlings should be planted in fairly deep holes, to encourage their roots to grow downwards. Cabbage has shallow roots, so be careful when cultivating not to hoe too deeply. Since cutworms sometimes attack cabbage seedlings — they will chew right through a stem and topple the plant — it's a good idea to give the plants paper "collars" when you set them out. Seeds should be planted at a depth of one-half inch. When seedlings appear, they should be thinned until there is a space of from eighteen to twenty inches between them. Fall cabbage is said to be larger than the spring varieties, so seeds planted for a fall harvest should be thinned until there is two feet between young plants. Spring and fall varieties benefit from regular light applications of fertilizer, preferably a fertilizer with a high percentage of nitrogen. Cabbage must be watered thoroughly and often. Mulching the crop will reduce the frequency with which you must water, since the mulch will retain moisture for the plants to draw on.

Unfortunately, cabbage seems to be very attractive to a variety of pests. The cabbage maggot is the larva of a tiny black fly that tunnels into the roots of a plant and causes it to wilt and even die. Several chemical dusts seem to be effective in eliminating this insect, which for some reason rarely troubles fall cabbage.

The green cabbage worm is a familiar pest. It feeds on a plant's leaves and tears large holes in them. Unchecked, it will burrow into and destroy the heads. If you inspect your garden regularly, you should be able to spot this pest, or at least the signs of its presence. Rotenone and sevin are among the poisons that can be used to control the pest. If the infestation seems very bad, you may have no alternative to spraying (see chapter 9 for a discussion of the use of pesticides.) Cabbage aphids generally appear only in the fall. They can be dislodged by directing a forceful stream of water onto each cabbage head.

Cabbage is ready to be harvested when a head is large and firm to the touch. Use a sharp knife to cut the stem just beneath the head. Try not to disturb the leaves of the plant, as it can still produce new, but smaller, heads.

Carrots

Carrots have a long growing season, require little cultivation, are resistant to most garden pests and diseases, and are an excellent source of vitamins, especially Vitamin A.

Carrot seeds can be sown as soon as the ground can be worked, and you can continue planting them until the first week of August. Where winters are mild, carrots can be sown until the end of September; this will insure a supply of fresh carrots throughout the winter. Depending on the variety of seed, and when it is sown, it should take between sixty-five and seventy-five days for carrots to mature. In winter, it takes several days longer.

When you open your first packet of carrot seeds, you may be surprised to find how tiny they are. Many gardeners mix carrot seeds with larger radish seeds and plant them together. Radishes grow faster than carrots and serve to indicate where the carrots are located. This makes cultivation easier, since the carrots are farther apart as a result and so require less thinning. By the time the radishes are ready to be harvested, the carrots should be thriving.

Carrots are said to prefer a loose, sandy soil, but will do quite well in any soil that has been deeply tilled and improved with compost or humus. Seeds should be planted one-half inch deep, at intervals of one-half inch. If you plant them in early spring, sow them on the south side of a board set on edge parallel with the row. The board will protect the seeds from chilling north or west winds. Remove the board when the weather turns warmer and the seedlings appear well established.

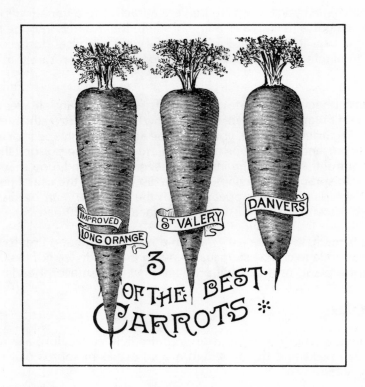

Seeds planted between the beginning of June and the end of August should be covered with an even layer of loose soil. Pour water directly on each seed before you cover it; don't water again until the seedlings appear. Rainfall, (unless heavy, prolonged, and accompanied by wind) will not disturb the cover greatly. The loose, dry surface soil serves to absorb some of the sun's intensity, but does not lessen its warmth. Too much light can burn carrot seeds and prevent them from germinating. But you must take care to keep the surface from hardening into a crust. So if there has been no rain for some time, cover the carrot rows with boards or sheets of plastic.

When the seedlings are visible, begin thinning them. Take great care as you weed around the carrots: their tops at first closely resemble weeds. (The radishes should help you to distinguish between friend and foe.) If the carrots

30

are to be large and well-formed, the plants should be spaced from one-and-one-half to two inches apart. Pull out any small, weak plants. The largest carrots will have the darkest, greenest tops; that's how you can tell when they are ready to be pulled. Sowing carrots three times during the spring and summer should provide a large crop. But if quantity is what you are after, seeds can be sown as often as every three weeks.

Carrot seedlings do best when given several light applications of fertilizer and when they receive regular waterings. Fertilizer should not be applied until seedlings have appeared, however: seeds can be badly burned by chemical fertilizers.

Carrots present few problems. Twisted carrots are caused by inadequate thinning. Carrots growing too closely together tend to grow towards and around one another. Forked roots occur when carrots encounter layers of soil too compact for them to penetrate and so have to grow around. Thorough cultivation before planting should prevent this.

Carrots are hardy, and are rarely affected by pests or diseases. The carrot rust fly can pose a problem, but is relatively uncommon. Eggs laid at the base of carrot leaves hatch into larvae. The tiny worms burrow into the root and make the carrot inedible. Leaves turning a rusty shade of brown indicate the presence of the pest. The rust fly occurs most frequently in warm weather. Carrots planted to reach full growth in cool weather will be free of infestations, as will those planted after June 1st. A layer of compost applied to the plants will not only benefit their growth, but will also encourage the presence of insect predators that feed on such pests as the rust fly.

To harvest carrots, grasp the leafy top and gently pull the carrot out of the soil. If the ground is hard, use a trowel to lever the roots out as you pull the tops. If the top snaps off, just dig the carrot up.

Celery

Celery is sometimes said to be difficult to grow. It isn't — if you pay heed to its specific requirements. These include a rich, loamy soil, at least four months of cool weather, plenty of moisture, and perhaps most important of all, lots of time and patience. In order for the plants to mature before the weather becomes very warm, start them indoors, in February or early March (in most parts of the country). Sow the seeds in a flat containing a soil mix of two parts humus and one part clean sand (for additional information, see Starting Plants Indoors). Place the seeds on the surface of the soil, at intervals of one-half inch, in rows spaced one-half inch apart, and sprinkle a light covering of sand over them. Immerse the flat in a container having sufficient water to reach half-way up the sides of the flat. When the soil surface feels damp to the touch, remove the flat from the container and allow it to drain. Keep the soil continuously moist, but not waterlogged, for the first two weeks. The flat should be placed in an airy (but not drafty), bright location.

The seedlings should be ready for transplanting into a larger flat in about a month. Plant them, in a similar soil mix, at intervals of two inches, in rows spaced two inches apart. In another month, they should be ready for transplanting. About two weeks before you plan to set them out, start exposing them for gradually lengthened periods to the air outdoors. Place the flats by an open window or door — but don't expose them to chilly drafts.

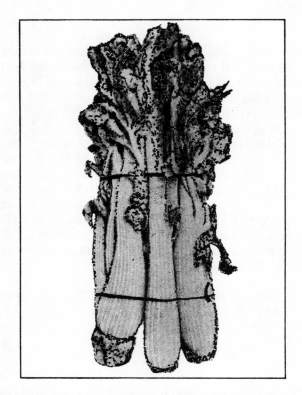

Begin preparing the soil where the celery will be planted about a week before your first scheduled transplant. Spade the soil up thoroughly, digging down about a foot, and mix in liberal amounts of organic materials and fertilizer. If there hasn't been any appreciable rain for a while, water the plot two to three days before you set out the seedlings. To provide the seedlings with a good start, the soil should be drenched to a depth of several inches, so make it a long and heavy watering.

Dig a trench for the seedlings, plant them in the bottom, and carefully pile up soil around them. Bring the soil up around the stem until as much of the stem remains above ground as when the seedlings were in their flat. The seedlings should be planted at intervals of six inches, in rows two feet apart. Weed the trenches frequently, and try to keep the ground continuously moist — though don't let it become waterlogged. Mulching the rows will eliminate most weeds, and reduce the frequency with which you must water. You can give the plants a light application of fertilizer every two weeks during the first six weeks. Though you may have used a fertilizer having a high percentage of nitrogen to treat the soil before planting, it's a good idea to use on the plants a fertilizer with a much lower concentration of that element. Hardwood ashes, rich in potash, and phosphate have a beneficial effect on the young plants.

Seeds for fall celery should be planted between the middle and the end of May. If the weather has been dry, soak the seeds in order to quicken germination. Initially the seeds should be covered by an inch of soil. When weeds begin to appear on top of the row, remove them so as not to disturb the soil excessively. After weeding, the seeds should still have a covering of at least a half-inch of soil, and when the seedlings are about two inches tall, give them a light application of fertilizer — pouring it on the soil around the plants. Give the young plants another week in this location, then transplant them to soil that has been spaded and treated with compost and a fertilizer. The plants should be eight to ten inches apart, in rows two feet apart. Fall celery can also be started in a coldframe. Once it has been transplanted, it should receive the same care as you have given your spring crop.

Insects rarely harm celery, and though blights and fungus infections may occur, they seem to be caused primarily by poor growing conditions. Plant your crop where there is plenty of sunlight, and adequate air and water drainage and you should have little, if any, trouble with diseases.

You can harvest several stalks from a head as they appear ready, or you can wait until the plant has formed a tight head, and remove the entire plant by cutting just above the roots. New stalks should grow from the roots, but will be smaller and less flavorful than the initial harvest.

Celery is certainly not the easiest of vegetables to raise. But the flavor and tenderness of fresh-picked celery, so unlike the kind you buy in a store, as well as your pride in a job well done, will make it well worth your effort.

Chard

I've included Swiss Chard in my list of vegetables for a first year garden because it is so easy to grow and yields such a high return. Six plants take up comparatively little space, but can produce for several months sufficient greens for a family of four.

Chard is a member of the beet family, but does not produce an edible root. It is grown only for its large, tender leaves.

Seeds should be planted at a depth of one-half inch, at intervals of an inch. The plants should be thinned until there is from seven to twelve inches between them (the leaves of the small plants you remove can be cooked and eaten). The plants will do their best in a sunny location and can adapt to most soil conditions, though they prefer a plot that is well-drained.

The plants should be given a light application of fertilizer once every three weeks. Some gardeners give them a dressing of compost. Chard roots may, even in a season, grow to a depth of six feet, so watering the leaves will be of no benefit. Give the soil around the plants several thorough soakings — the frequency will depend on the amount of rain during the season.

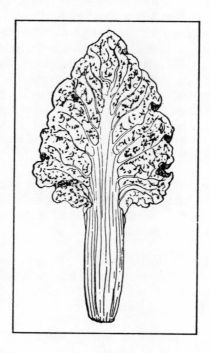

Chard seems to be resistant to all common vegetable diseases and most pests. Aphids occasionally attack it, but you can drive them away by aiming your hose at the leaves.

There are two methods of harvesting. Some gardeners remove only the outer leaves and allow new leaves from the center of the plant to grow outwards. This way one plant may be harvested again and again throughout the summer. Other gardeners claim that the largest, outer leaves are too tough. They cut the plant down, and mix the small, new leaves and older, larger leaves together. You may want to try both methods, and decide for yourself which is preferable. When cooked, the leaves should be tender and delicately flavored.

Chard planted in the spring requires sixty to sixty-five days to mature. Seeds planted during the summer require perhaps forty-five to fifty days. Unless your region suffers from especially harsh winters, you can cover chard plants with a thick layer of straw or mulch, and continue harvesting leaves throughout the winter. How many vegetables are that versatile?

Chard also makes an excellent container plant. Potted in a tub large enough to have a soil depth of one to two feet, chard can give you a long, large yield of greens.

Corn

Corn is a favorite of mine, but you won't find it growing in my garden. That's because in my backyard space is at a premium, and a few stalks of corn return a modest yield for the amount of space they occupy. Moreover, where I live, corn takes most of the summer to mature; that means I can only plant a hardy fall crop in the space where the corn has stood. But many gardeners will make any sacrifice to bring in a crop of corn. If you have a large garden plot, planting corn will call for no sacrifice, and you will have the pleasure of harvesting and eating corn far fresher and sweeter than any you have tasted before.

Corn needs plenty of sunlight and moisture. It grows in almost any consistency of soil, but a light, sandy loam, which absorbs both water and warmth readily, seems best.

Mix a large load of compost into the site you have marked off for corn. Before you plant the seeds or seedlings, treat the soil with a dressing of a complete fertilizer, mixing it in at a depth of from three to four inches.

Plant the seeds four inches apart, at a depth of one to two inches, using your fingers or a trowel to gently tamp in soil over the seeds. The rows should be between 32 and 42 inches apart. Because of the way in which corn is pollinated, it is best to plant several short rows rather than one long row.

To assure yourself of a steady supply of fresh corn, plant another row each week for several weeks, or plant seeds of early, midsummer, and late varieties at the same time. It's a good idea to sow corn on either the northern or the eastern sides of your garden. Remember: your corn will eventually be quite tall; if the plants are located on the southern end of your garden, they will prevent sunlight from reaching your other crops.

When the seedlings are eight to ten inches high, thin the rows, until there is an interval of from eight to twelve inches between plants. Weeds can be destructive competitors for corn seedlings, so keep the rows free of them. Use a hoe to weed the rows once a week for the first two months the seeds are in the ground. After that, the stalks should be tall enough to deprive the weeds of sunlight. When you use any tool around corn seedlings or mature corn plants, use it gently; be careful to cultivate only the surface of the soil: the roots of corn plants remain quite near the surface. You can also apply a mulch of hay or straw between the rows immediately after you have sown the seeds, to prevent weeds from appearing and to make an additional supply of nutrients available to the seedlings. When the plants are eight inches high, apply a layer of mulch between them. After the corn has been harvested, turn the mulch under to improve the soil for a fall crop, or allow it to remain on the surface for the winter, where it will serve as a ground cover.

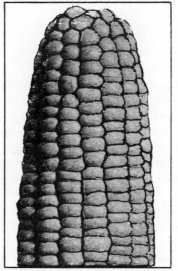

Corn grows very rapidly once it has sprouted, so you will have to supply it with regular applications of fertilizer. When the plants are a foot tall, dress either side of the rows with a complete fertilizer. Rake it into the soil. Well rotted animal manure and cottonseed or soya meal, mixed in equal portions, can also be applied around the rows.

Corn needs plenty of water. Water the ground before you sow the seeds, and water it again when the seedlings are four inches tall. After that, whenever the soil around the rows feels dry to a depth of four inches, give the plants water. You can use a sprinkler, or a hose with a spray nozzle. Water in the morning, and water thoroughly — but don't allow the ground to become waterlogged.

Corn suffers if it stays on the stalk too long. Ears should be harvested as soon as they feel firm and the kernels appear to be filled out. If a milky liquid appears when you probe a kernel with your fingernail, the ear is at the peak of its freshness. A clear liquid indicates that it will take several more days for the ear to mature. And a viscous white material means that the ear has remained on the stalk too long. To remove an ear, grip it near its base and, using a twisting, downward motion, break it from the stalk. As soon as an ear is removed, its natural sugar will begin turning into starch, so don't pick an ear until you are ready to use it. But if you can't cook, can, or freeze an ear as soon as it is picked, drop it in a container of ice water; that will slow the sugar-to-starch conversion.

After all the ears have been removed from the stalk, pull the stalks out and shred them for your compost heap. Or till them into the soil. Or dig a shallow hole close to the garden, and bury the stalks under several inches of soil. The nutrients in the decomposing stalks are too valuable just to throw away.

Corn is affected by few diseases and only two persistent or common pests, the corn borer and the earworm. The borers, about an inch long, feed on both stalks and ears. If you discover any on a stalk, pick them off and destroy them. Diazinon is said to control infestations of borers, but I would hesitate to use it in a home garden. (For further information on pests and pest remedies, see chapter 9). Earworms hatch from eggs laid on cornstalks by a moth. When they hatch, they can rapidly chew away patches of kernels on every ear found on a stalk. One-quarter of a teaspoon of mineral oil, applied to each stalk with a medicine dropper, will kill the eggs before any earworms can hatch. Rotenone and Sevin can also be used to end an earworm attack — but only when the pests are present in large numbers.

Cucumbers

Cucumbers should not be planted until the soil has warmed. If you live in a region of short summers, give the plants a head start by planting seeds in pots indoors four to six weeks before the soil is warm enough for them. In most regions, this will be by late May.

The best place to plant cucumbers is where last year's bean patch was; the seeds and seedlings both can use the reservoir of nitrogen the beans will have left in the soil. Of course, you won't have such an opportunity your first year, but the practice is worth keeping in mind for the following spring. Cucumbers seem to do better on flat ground than on a slope — probably because a greater amount of moisture sinks into level ground, and to keep growing, cucumbers need a steady supply of water.

Many gardeners treat the soil where they plan to sow cucumbers with a dressing of seasoned manure or compost. The seeds should be planted at a depth of one inch, at three-inch intervals in the row. The rows should be at least five feet apart, to allow space for the vines. If space is at a premium, you can "train" the vines to grow on a trellis. Cucumbers love sun, so it's a good idea to plant them in rows facing east to west.

As soon as the plants are three to four inches above the ground, start cultivating. In fact, to keep the soil loose, you will have to cultivate the rows at least once a week. A hardened surface will retard the plant's growth. The rows should be thinned until there is a foot between plants.

When the vines are at least eighteen inches long apply a dressing of fertilizer to the sides of each row. Should the elements cooperate, apply the food during a light summer rain; the water will mix with and carry the fertilizer immediately into the soil.

Mature plants will have roots up to three feet long, and since the plant takes in moisture through its roots, watering the foliage will have little positive effect on the plants. Many gardeners dig irrigation trenches alongside the rows. You may not want to go to such trouble, especially if you have only a few plants. In that case, heavy watering of the soil every three weeks (more frequently, if the summer is very dry) should be sufficient.

About seven weeks after sowing, small cucumbers will appear. Cucumbers can be picked when they are as short as three inches or as long as eight inches. Pick them before they turn yellow; yellowing indicates the fruit is hardening. Keep the vines clear of mature cucumbers; if even one or two is left on a plant, that plant will not produce any others. When you harvest, make sure to hold out the vines, which are fragile and can break easily. Twist the fruit gently with your hand, or use a small sharp knife to cut it off; be careful not to cut the vine — only the short stem attaching the cucumber to the vine.

Cucumber beetles pose a double-barreled threat to your cucumbers: not only do they burrow among and damage the plant's roots, but are also likely to introduce bacterial wilt, a disease for which there is no certain cure. The beetles generally attack only immature plants, so while your plants are still young, keep a close watch over them for symptoms. Several insecticides are said to be effective against the pest. Cucumbers once were vulnerable to a variety of diseases, but growers have succeeded in producing seeds resistant to most infections. You can read your seed packet for details.

Cucumbers are available in a remarkable array of sizes and shapes. If you simply don't have the room to grow cucumbers outdoors, there are several excellent miniature varieties that can be grown in tubs or hanging baskets indoors, or even on the ground if you have a small piece of ground for them outdoors.

Eggplant

Eggplant needs between 100 and 130 days to grow to maturity. This means that in most areas you will have to give the plants a head start on the growing season by beginning them indoors. If you cannot raise the seedlings in your house, a hotbed will provide an excellent alternative. And if you simply cannot raise the plants yourself, you can purchase seedlings at many garden centers.

If you are growing the plants from seed, use flats or pots filled with a sterile soil mix, sphagnum moss or vermiculite. Place the seeds at a depth of half an inch. You will have to maintain a soil temperature no lower than 70° (preferably around 75°) until the seeds have sprouted. (For further information, see Starting Plants Indoors).

Don't move the seedlings outdoors until the soil has noticeably warmed, and all danger of frost has passed. About a week before you anticipate transplanting the seedlings, begin exposing them to the air by placing the flats on a windowsill or by carrying them outside for gradually longer periods of time. This exposure will serve to "harden them off," so they do not go into shock when they are transplanted.

Before transplanting the seedlings, treat the soil where you intend to plant them with a heavy dressing of compost, well rotted manure and a substantial dose of a complete fertilizer. Dig a row of shallow holes, at intervals of from 30 to 36 inches. Give the ground a through watering, and after the water drains into the ground, bring the seedlings out. Brush the soil gently up around the stem. To protect the plants from a cutworm attack, loosely fasten a paper collar around the stem, leaving half of the collar above ground.

Keep the rows clear of weeds. If you prefer not to weed, use a light mulch to cover the ground all around the plants. Water frequently, but moderately. If you use a mulch you should have to water less frequently, since the mulch, by shielding the ground, will slow the rate of evaporation. If the plants just don't look healthy, give them another dose of fertilizer. Use a complete fertilizer. But even if you think you have reason to keep feeding the plants, don't do so more frequently than every 35 days.

Eggplants can produce a number of fruits. But the more fruits each plant produces, the smaller they are. Allow no more than six fruits to form on each plant. Pick off any additional tip shoots or blossoms. When the fruits are a dark, glossy purple, and about six inches long, use a sharp knife to sever the fruit from the plant, cutting just below the point where the stem joins the fruit. Wear gloves during the procedure; the stems are rather prickly. If a fruit stops growing and loses its sheen, remove and discard it. There may yet be sufficient time for another fruit to form.

The eggplant lacebug, the Colorado potato beetle, and the hornworm may all attack eggplants. Treat the lacebug with a Malathion spray. Pick off and destroy the hornworms, and potato beetles. If an infestation of the beetles continues, a spray of Rotenone or Sevin should prove effective. Allow at least five days to pass after you have sprayed before harvesting any fruit.

The only disease that regularly occurs in eggplants is a wilt that also affects tomatoes and potatoes. If you avoid planting eggplants where the other two crops have been during the previous three years, you can greatly reduce the chance of this wilt occuring. Eggplant does present some problems but you will find the flavor and versatility of it well worth the effort.

Kale

Kale has to be one of the hardiest of all vegetables. It can be grown during the summer, but seems to prefer cool weather. Indeed, gardeners in northern regions have reported harvesting crops of tasty kale from under several feet of snow! Kale can adapt to most soil types and, in a relatively small space, will produce quantities of vitamin-rich greens.

It can be planted anytime from early spring until a month before the first projected frost date. But seed should not be sown during very hot weather, since it will rarely grow under such conditions. Many gardeners don't plant kale until late summer; then they sow it in the area previously occupied by beans or peas. This is an excellent idea, because the beans will have enriched the soil with nitrogen, and if it is to do really well, kale needs fertile soil.

Kale can be grown in soil types ranging from a light, sandy consistency to a heavy clay, but it requires a steady supply of nutrients to mature. To provide the necessary supply, distribute lime and compost over the surface of the area you intend to plant. Mix them thoroughly into the soil. Place the seeds in one-half inch deep depressions, and gently brush the soil over them. Seeds should be placed in the row at intervals of six inches, and the rows should be from twenty-four to thirty inches apart. Plants should be thinned until they are from sixteen to twenty-four inches apart.

When the plants are two or three inches high, dress the soil around them with humus or compost, giving the ground to within three inches of the seedlings a light, even application. Don't pack it around the stem or you may burn the plant badly.

Kale has a shallow root system that spreads horizontally just a few inches below the surface. This means the plants have to be watered frequently; to develop, kale needs a regular supply of moisture, and the roots simply aren't deep enough to tap that moisture found well below the surface. Don't water the foliage — water the soil. Remember, a plant draws in moisture through its roots, not through its leaves.

Some gardeners apply a mulch to kale. A mulch conserves moisture in the soil, and protects soil and plant roots from intense summer heat. Evaporation is thus slowed down. The mulch will also act as a source of additional nutrients.

You can harvest a plant by cutting it at the base — but most gardeners I've spoken to prefer to remove only as many leaves as they need, and to let the plant keep growing. The large outer leaves are too tough for human consumption, but the younger, slightly smaller leaves are quite tasty and rich in vitamins. Cook them as you would spinach, or else add them to other dishes as a garnish. The tiny new leaves can be mixed in a salad or added to soups. When you leave the plant in the ground, taking only what you need, it will continue to yield tender greens right through the winter. An experienced gardener living in New England swears that the taste and consistency of the leaves are much improved by cold weather and an occasional covering of snow.

Aphids and several types of beetles are prone to attack kale. Healthy plants seem much less vulnerable to attack. So proper care of your crop alone may prevent some attacks. Beetles can be removed by picking them off, and a stream of water directed on the underside of the leaves and along the stems will knock most aphids off. (For additional information on dealing with pests in the garden see chapter 9).

Lettuce

Lettuce is justly popular among home gardeners. It is easy to grow, is hardy enough to withstand the low temperatures of spring and early fall nights, and can adapt to almost any consistency of soil, so long as it is supplied with regular applications of organic matter. Many varieties of lettuce are available, so you should have no trouble finding one that's especially well-suited to your taste and gardening circumstances.

Generally speaking, there are four types of lettuce, and each type features many varieties. Head, or Iceberg, lettuce is the kind most frequently sold in stores and so is probably the most familiar type. As it matures it forms a small, tight head. Leaf lettuce varieties produce large, loose heads that tend to separate into large leaves. These leaves may be removed as needed, and the head left to continue growing. Butterhead varieties form soft heads that are composed of yellow leaves that are more loosely folded around one another. The outer leaves of the head are darker than those near the center. Cos, or Romaine, lettuce forms tall, elongated heads having tightly folded leaves.

Lettuce is among the first vegetables you can plant in the spring. In fact, you can harvest a crop by early summer if you start the plants indoors during the first week in March. Sow seeds in flats or in a coldframe. Treat the seeds as you would any other vegetable (See Starting Plants Indoors). By early April, the plants should be at least three inches tall. Harden them off by placing them on the windowsill of an opened window, gradually increasing the length of their exposure by several minutes each day for a week.

The plants should be spaced between a foot and a foot-and-a-half apart. The rows should be about two feet apart. If you are unable or unwilling to start plants indoors, you can sow seeds in the ground by mid-April in most areas. The seeds should be placed a quarter-of-an-inch below the surface, at intervals of an inch, in rows one-and-one-half feet apart. When the seedlings are two inches high, thin the rows so that there is an interval of two inches between plants. When the plants start to crowd one another, thin the rows again until there is a space of six inches between plants. Thin the plants again, in one or two weeks, so that they are at least a foot apart. For this last thinning, you can either discard the plants you remove, or transplant them to another row.

Lettuce roots are very shallow. The seedlings and roots especially are very small, and very close to the surface. So you must keep the rows free of weeds. A weed that would not affect the seedling of another vegetable can destroy a young lettuce plant. A light mulch of humus placed all around the plants should keep down most weeds, as well as provide additional nutrients for the plants.

Precisely because they are so shallow, lettuce roots cannot draw on the quantities of nutrients stored deeper in the soil. So before you sow seeds, or transplant seedlings, work a load of organic material into the spot selected for lettuce. Give the seeds or seedlings a light application of fertilizer, by mixing the food into the soil around the plants. Give the plants another feeding when they are half grown (you can determine when that will be by consulting the seed packet — it should give you the number of weeks required for the plants to reach maturity). Because plants draw in nutrients through their roots, and not through their leaves, it is useless to apply fertilizer directly onto a plant. Indeed, such an action could prove harmful, as the leaves might be damaged by the solution. Bear in mind, moreover, that in the case of leaf crops, anything you put on the plant may end up inside of you.

Lettuce roots are also easy to disturb and to damage. This is again because they are so shallow. Be especially careful when using tools in or around the rows of lettuce. Use hoes, rakes, and trowels only on the surface soil — don't dig into the ground near a plant. Water the lettuce lightly, but frequently. Don't depend on rainfall to do the job. Establish a watering schedule for the crop, and try to stick to it. Once the weather has turned warm, a light watering twice a week should prove just about right.

Lettuce is not adapted to hot weather. In fact, the high temperatures common to most areas in midsummer can cause lettuce to "bolt" — that is, to go to seed. Most gardeners I have spoken to plant one crop for harvesting in early summer, and sow another in late July or early August for harvesting in the fall. Gardeners who have cold frames or hotbeds can provide their families with fresh lettuce throughout the winter.

Lettuce must be used soon after it is harvested, so it's a good idea to stagger your planting; otherwise, you might find your entire crop maturing at the same time, providing you with more lettuce than you can possibly consume — unless you start eating it three times a day. Divide the seeds you intend to plant into three portions, and sow a portion every ten days in flats or in the ground. This way, you will be able to avoid being burdened at any one time with too much lettuce.

Most varieties of lettuce are harvested by severing the stem of the plant close to the ground, though the leaf varieties are harvested a leaf at a time or as need dictates. New leaves should continue to appear. Heads of lettuce, however, should be harvested when the center feels firm.

Cabbageworms, aphids, slugs, and snails sometimes attack lettuce. The worms will be large enough for you to locate and pick off. Aphids can be dislodged by directing a focused stream of water onto the heads by means of a hose or a watering can. Snails and slugs can also be removed by hand. Neither should pose a serious problem. I don't recommend the use of chemicals on lettuce leaves because, as mentioned above, that's what you and your family will be eating. Once a chemical has been sprayed on a plant, it's extremely difficult to remove its residue. So don't apply anything to the leaves except water. Lettuce is rarely troubled with serious pest or disease problems. Fulfill the cultural requirements of the plant, and you're unlikely to encounter any problems.

Onions

Of the commoner garden vegetables, onions come closest to being indestructible. They prefer a soil treated with manure and fertilizer, but seem to adapt to practically any other soil. Cool weather — even an occasional frost — has little effect on them, few diseases or pests trouble them, and if all that is not sufficient to recommend them, they require only a modest amount of space to return a high yield.

You can start onion plants from seed, or you can purchase onion seedlings, or you can use "sets." "Sets," which you can get at garden centers, are the small bulbs of several varieties of onions. They produce a mature crop of onions much earlier than seeds. Sets should be planted four inches apart in one-inch deep trenches. There should be at least a foot of space between trenches. One end of a set will have a noticeable point. Place each set in the trench with the pointed end facing upwards. Fill the trenches in, gently tamping soil over and around the sets. Seedlings, which can also be had at garden centers, can be planted in much the same way as sets. Place them four inches apart in two-inch deep trenches. Both sets and seedlings can be planted as soon as the ground can be worked.

Whether you plant seeds, sets, or seedlings, you should first treat the location with well rotted manure or compost. Mix the materials thoroughly into the soil.

And before you plant, apply a complete fertilizer to the ground. Onions seem especially to appreciate quantities of phosphorus and potassium — so use a fertilizer high in these elements.

Onion seeds sprout most successfully in cool soil, as do sets and seedlings; plant them as soon as the soil can be worked. Use plenty of seeds, placing them in depressions one-quarter of an inch deep. Over the first three or four weeks, thin the plants once, and then again. The seedlings should stand four inches apart. Because onion seedlings are rather slow to appear, you may want to mix some radish seeds in the rows. The radishes will appear before the onions, and will help you to identify the locations of the rows.

When weeds proliferate around onions, the onions are generally the losers. Hoe the rows frequently, but lightly. Don't dig the hoe down into the soil. Using a chopping motion, bring it down across the surface. You'll probably have to get down and hand-pick weeds as well. When the plants are eight inches high, apply a dressing of a complete fertilizer along the rows, and work it into the soil with a rake. Don't push the fertilizer closely around the stem. To produce very large onions, you will have to gently brush or shovel soil away from the bulb, until only the bottom third of the developing bulb is underground. This exposure gives the onion plenty of room to expand. Be careful while exposing the bulb not to strike it with any sharp surface.

When the tops bend over the bulbs, turning brown at that point where they brush against the bulb, it is time to harvest the onion. Grasp the top, pull the bulb firmly, but gently, out of the ground. And now you'll discover another of the onion's attractions. It is one of the easiest vegetables to store.

Brush any clots of soil off of the roots. Then spread the onions out on a clean surface, where the sun can reach them. They should remain exposed to the sun and air for several days — but bring them under cover if rain is likely; bulbs that are soaked are useless. Remove the tops, and store the bulbs in a cool dry place.

The only insect to pose a serious problem to onions is the onion maggot, a tiny white insect that chews its way into the bulb. Radishes, planted on either side of a row of onions, are said to repel the insect. If a plant seems badly damaged, pull it out and destroy it — don't add it to your compost heap.

Onion thrips settle on the leaves of the plant. If the leaves of the plant develop white blotches, suspect thrips. If the damage is minor, remove the affected leaves. If the leaves have become wilted and badly blotched, remove the bulb. A spray of Diazinon is said to be effective against the pest, but most home gardeners will never have an infestations of thrips serious enough to call for such a powerful poison. Never apply any chemical to onions within three weeks of the anticipated harvest date.

Peas

Peas are especially suitable for the home gardener. They require a minimal amount of care, are resistant to diseases and rarely bothered by pests, and actually improve the soil they have been planted in. Peas are a "nitrogen fixing" crop: this means they collect and store more of that vital element than they can use. By tilling the plants back into the soil after you have picked the last pod, or by pulling the plants out and adding them to your compost heap, you can return a valuable supply of nitrogen to your garden. Almost any crop will benefit from an increased supply of nitrogen, but some vegetables need especially large amounts of it in order to produce healthy crops. It is wise, therefore, to rotate your crops in such a way as to take advantage of the bonus left by last year's nitrogen-fixing crops.

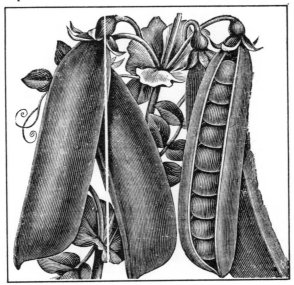

Peas are a cool weather crop. Plant the seeds as early in the spring as you can — that is, as soon as the ground is warm enough to be worked. "Dwarf" varieties take about 55 days to reach maturity. "Tall-growing," pole varieties have longer vines, and produce larger pods in greater numbers, but take at least 70 days to mature.

The depth at which peas should be planted depends on the consistency of soil in your garden. If yours is a "heavy" soil, the seeds should be placed an inch below the surface. If your soil is "light," they should be planted in depressions two inches deep. By working organic materials or a compost into the soil before you plant, you can "lighten" it, and at the same time increase the amount of nutrients available to the seeds and improve the ability of the soil to accept water without becoming waterlogged.

Before planting the seeds, they should be soaked in water and allowed to "sprout," that is, to develop their first roots. This procedure will give the seeds a "head start" when they are planted. If the seeds are to be sown in an area where peas have not previously been grown, it's a good idea to treat them with an "inoculant," a bacterial mixture that will aid the young plants in the process of drawing in nitrogen from the air. A small container of the mixture will be all you need for even a large garden. It is available at garden supply centers, and from some mail-order suppliers.

The seeds of "dwarf" varieties should be planted at intervals of an inch, in one or more rows. Some gardeners have one long row of peas; others plant several shorter rows. The length and number of the rows depends on the size and shape of your plot. When the seedlings appear, thin the rows so that the plants have two to three inches separating them. Pole varieties can be planted in wide rows or in double rows spaced one-and-a-half feet apart. Sow the seeds at intervals of two to two-and-a-half inches. After the seedlings appear, the rows should be thinned until there is a distance of four inches between plants. The rows of pole varieties must be kept free of weeds. Cultivate frequently, or else mulch the rows after the seeds have been planted. Because "tall-growing" peas climb upwards as they grow, you must provide support for the vines, either of close-meshed wire or wood. Erect the supports between two rows as soon as you have planted the seeds. The supports should be at least four feet tall.

Aside from weeding, peas don't require much care. One month after planting, dissolve a water-soluble fertilizer and apply it to the rows. Because they are planted so early in the spring, few diseases or pests should trouble your peas. Pea aphids can infest and destroy a crop of immature peas, but seem to appear most frequently on late-growing crops. Spring peas are rarely attacked. Sprays are available that should quickly curtail the problem. Root rot may attack the plants, but this seems to occur only when the crop has been damaged in some way. Waterlogged ground causes roots to become soft and pulpy, and vulnerable to this infection. Dressing the plants with a strong, undiluted fertilizer can also damage the roots, and provide the opportunity for the infection to enter a plant. Peas are so hardy that most problems are caused by mistakes we make. If promptly corrected, such mistakes need not be fatal to your crop.

Many first-time gardeners make the mistake of allowing pods to remain too long on the vine. This would seem to make good sense: the pod seems to keep growing, and the peas can only keep on getting bigger, right? Bigger, and tougher: pods harden rapidly after they reach maturity, and as they harden the peas lose their flavor. Harvest the pods when they have turned a light green, and have acquired a rather round shape. Snap the pods off, firmly but gently. Don't tear the pods loose; you can damage and even kill a plant by such careless picking. If you plan to use peas the day you pick them, don't pick them until you are ready to shell and cook them. If you must pick what you need ahead of time, don't shell the peas until just before cooking. The longer the period between harvesting and cooking, the less sweet the peas will be, since the sugar in them will begin turning to starch about two hours after harvesting. Peas can be frozen or canned and will retain their sweetness.

Peppers

There are two kinds of peppers, sweet and hot, and many varieties of each, in a wide range of sizes, shapes, and shades. The fruits of almost all peppers are green while immature, turning increasingly red as they approach maturity. Peppers differ from most other vegetables in that they can be eaten at almost any stage of development after their appearence on a plant.

Sweet (also known as bell) peppers grow on short, large-leafed bushes. Hot pepper plants are taller and have smaller leaves. Sweet peppers mature in about eighty days. Hot peppers take even longer to reach maturity, and so are best grown in areas having long, warm summers.

Peppers are vulnerable to cold, so it's advisable to begin a plant indoors about two months before the onset of summer, or to purchase seedlings. The seeds should be planted in flats or pots, at a depth of from a quarter to an eighth of an inch below the surface. The pots or flats should be kept in a hotbed, under fluorescent lights or on a very sunny windowsill. The temperature of the air around the seedlings should never fall lower than seventy degrees, even at night. When the seedlings develop their first pairs of leaves transplant them to larger containers, spacing the plants two inches apart. Keep the soil moist, but don't water so much or so often as to make the soil waterlogged.

When all danger of frost has passed, and the days have turned warm, transplant the seedlings into the garden. Give them a sunny location, spacing the plants one-and-one-half to two feet apart. If you have more than one row of peppers, space the rows two to three feet apart. However, unless you or your family have a lasting appetite for peppers, four or five plants will supply all you need, and possibly more. If you are interested in peppers only as an occasional addition to your diet, two plants will suffice.

They needn't go into your vegetable garden. You can plant them in a flower bed, to obtain a colorful, unusual contrast with the blooms of your ornamentals. If you're really pressed for space, you can even plop them down by a row of shrubs. As long as it can get sufficient sunlight, a pepper plant can adapt to almost any location.

It can also adapt to almost any kind of soil. Warmth and abundant sunlight are its primary needs. A light dressing of a ''complete'' fertilizer every thirty days should supply all the additional nutrients the plant requires. During very dry periods, water the plants twice a week. Unless rain occurs frequently, water the plants thoroughly once a week. You may want to apply a mulch around the plants (grass clippings will do a very good job), to keep down weeds and to retain a steady supply of moisture for the roots to draw upon.

For a vegetable so sensitive to temperatures, peppers are otherwise remarkably hardy. Few insects or diseases threaten them. Cutworms may slash through seedlings just after they have been set out in the garden, but this can be avoided by placing a cardboard collar around the stem of the plant, to protect the portions of the stem just under and just above the ground.

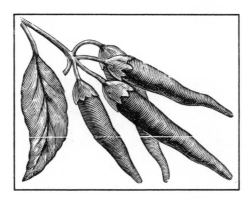

Leaf mosaic is the only disease that strikes pepper plants with any frequency. An infected plant appears stunted, and will feature misshapen, blotched leaves. Growth ceases, and the plant generally dies quite rapidly. Once a plant is infected, there is little you can do. As soon as you are certain that the plant's appearence matches the symptoms of leaf mosaic, pull it out and destroy it. It is a highly contagious disease, and can spread from plant to plant by even the most fleeting contact: so before you go back into the garden, wash your hands, gloves, and any tools used to dig up and dispose of an infected plant. Mosaic is deadly, but does not seem to be a common problem. Your county agricultural agent may be able to inform you of outbreaks of specific plant diseases in your area, and suggest some preventative measures (for further information on diseases, see chapter 9).

Sweet peppers are picked when they have reached a desirable size (varying with the intended use of the pepper). They may be harvested while still green and immature, or when they have ripened and turned red. Mature peppers are said to have a higher Vitamin C content than that of green peppers. Sweet peppers can be stuffed, sliced for salads, or used as an ingredient in cooked dishes. Hot peppers are used as a spice, and as an ingredient in many international recipes. Both sweet and hot peppers should be cut from a plant, not pulled or torn away. Use a sharp knife to cut through the stem one-half inch from the point where it joins the fruit. If you are harvesting hot peppers, remember not to rub your hand over your eye; the juice will act as an irritant. If you will be handling a number of hot peppers, wear gloves.

Potatoes

Potatoes are not at all temperamental. Once planted, they require little care. Yet they usually return a high yield per garden foot. If you don't have the space or inclination to grow a large crop of potatoes, I recommend that you raise perhaps two or three plants in some unused corner or odd space in your garden. The taste of a home-grown potato, especially a tender young potato picked before it is fully grown, is reward enough for any difficulty you might encounter in fitting the plants in.

You don't grow potatoes from seed, or from seedlings. To start a potato, you plant a potato: that is, you plant a section of a potato that has gone to seed. If you don't quickly use a store-bought potato, or if it is stored improperly, it develops sprouts, commonly called eyes. It is from the eyes that new plants grow. You can buy seed potatoes from many mail order seed companies. Some garden supply centers also stock them. I don't recommend purchasing potatoes and allowing them to sprout: the seed potatoes available in stores or through the mail have been treated to be disease resistant — and potatoes are unfortunately vulnerable to a variety of maladies.

Potatoes thrive in a well drained soil that is slightly acidic. Work a load of well-rotted manure into the spot you've selected for the crop about two weeks before planting. Keep the seed potatoes in a cool place until you are ready to plant them. Many gardeners plant potatoes twice during the growing season, once in late April or early May, and again in late May. The first planting should mature in late August or early September, and can be consumed right away. The second will mature in late September, and most of it can be stored for later use.

If the seed potatoes have not been sliced into portions, use a clean knife to do so twenty-four hours before you intend to plant them. Each section should have at least two eyes, with a generous amount of flesh surrounding the eyes. During the first stage of growth, the flesh will have to supply the nutrients the eyes require.

Place the sections in individual holes, or in a trench, dug to a depth of five inches. Cover each with soil until a slight mound is created. The sections should be placed at intervals of a foot, and if you have more than one row, the rows should be at least a foot-and-a-half apart. Plant only on a warm day, and when the soil is dry: wet soil will cause the sections to rot before they have a chance to develop. Plant as early in the spring as you can, since potatoes have a lengthy growing season.

Keep the soil in and around the rows loose and free of weeds. Cultivate shallowly; the roots lie quite close to the surface. If you can find a sufficient supply of mulch, apply a layer of it a foot thick over the rows; it will kill off all the weeds, and provide additional nutrients for the plants.

Another method of growing calls for clearing an area ten feet square. Loosen the soil, and spread sections ten inches apart all across the surface. Then cover the entire area with a layer of mulch one to one-and-a-half feet thick. (This method calls for a lot of mulch — more than may be readily available to you.) The plants will grow right up through the mulch, and the potatoes will form in the mulch as if they were growing beneath the ground. To remove individual potatoes, all you need do is reach down and gently pull them out. In September, carefully rake back the mulch and harvest the remainder of the crop. I haven't tried this method, but have been assured by those who have that it works.

When the seedlings first appear above the ground, brush additional soil over them until they have been entirely covered. Do this each time the tops appear, until you have an eight to ten inch mound running the length of the row. This hilling provides plenty of very loose soil for the plants, and makes it easier for the developing potatoes to grow and expand. It also serves to protect your first planting from a late frost. Throughout the summer, keep the potatoes covered with soil, since sunlight can quickly turn them green and inedible. Water the rows once or twice a week — varying the frequency with the amount of rainfall that week. If the rows have been mulched, you won't have to water so much.

You can pick young potatoes by midsummer — their taste is especially sweet and delicate. To harvest the bulk of the crop, take a spading fork and carefully loosen the soil around the row. Pick a sunny day to harvest the crop, when soil will be dry and the potatoes easier to remove. Slide the fork under the main stem of a plant, lift it, and gently shake the potatoes free. Do this as gently as possible: potatoes bruise easily. Don't allow them to remain in the sun: take them to your kitchen or to a storage area as soon as they have been harvested.

Early varieties of potatoes indicate maturity by sending forth flowers on their vines. Later varieties are said to be ready for harvesting when the vines yellow and appear to have dried out.

Store in a cool, dark area any potatoes you do not intend to use immediately. Brush away any soil remaining on the tubers, but don't wash them until you are ready to cook them. A "good" storage potato is said to be one on which the skin will not loosen when it is rubbed. If the skin comes away in your hand, according to this rough rule, the potato should be used as soon as possible.

Potatoes require relatively little care to grow, but may require a good deal of time to defend, for many garden pests seem irresitibly drawn to them. One benefit of mulching is the protection it affords the crop — few pests can or will penetrate the mulch in order to attack.

"Late blight" and "common scab" are the diseases most frequently appearing on potatoes. Several applications of compost, mixed into the soil around the rows at weekly intervals after the seedlings have appeared will give some protection. Compost increases the acidity of the soil, and the more acidic the soil, the less likely it is that an infection will occur. There is also a spray available that is said to give a crop some protection from these diseases. Because tomatoes are vulnerable to the same diseases, they should never be planted in a spot last occupied by potatoes. The development of disease resistant potato varieties has reduced the frequency of infections.

Radish

Radishes are not only easy to grow; they also grow remarkably fast, maturing in as little as twenty-five days. As mentioned at several points in these profiles, they can be used to indicate the locations and dimensions of other, slower growing crops. Don't plant your radishes in rows — mix the seeds in with other crops, and sow them throughout your garden.

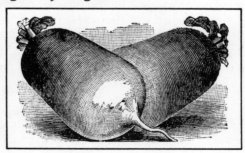

Radishes are a cool weather crop, so seeds should be sown as soon as the ground can be worked. If you're fond of radishes, you can continue sowing at two week intervals until midsummer, resuming again in August. (Very warm weather causes radishes to go to seed.) A light application of a complete fertilizer, worked into the ground before planting, seems to benefit the plants. Apparently because they grow so rapidly, they need nutrients almost immediately. The seeds should be placed in depressions one-quarter-of-an-inch deep, and about one inch apart. There should be between a foot and a foot-and-a-half between rows, or groupings of radishes. Because their roots remain just below the surface, be careful if you are cultivating around radishes not to hoe deeply. Radishes planted in the summer should be placed three-quarters-of-an-inch below the surface, to afford them greater protection from excessive warmth. Thin summer radishes until they are two to three inches apart. Radishes planted for a fall harvest should be sown three-quarters-of-an-inch deep, and the seedlings should be thinned until there is an interval of five to six inches between them. Midseason and fall varieties generally require more time to mature than spring varieties.

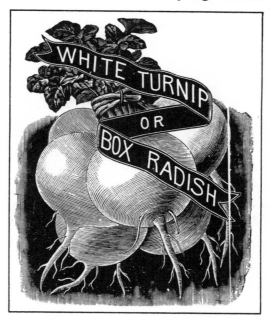

Radishes seem to do everything but weed themselves. They'll need you to do that, and you should try to keep the area around radishes weed free. They don't require frequent waterings. If there has been no rain, water them once a week. They shouldn't need more than the initial application of fertilizer. Few pests, and no diseases, affect them. Indeed, some gardeners plant radishes purposefully to attract insects that might otherwise attack some other root crop — onions, for instance.

You can begin pulling radishes when they appear to be slightly larger than peas. Winter radishes generally reach greater dimensions than either spring or midsummer varieties. Cracked or split radishes, or radishes with a very pungent odor, have been left in the ground too long, and should not be eaten. Toss them onto your compost pile. You can store fall radishes by placing them in a well drained trench lined with straw. Cover them with a layer of earth, a layer of soil, and a final layer of earth. Such storage is most successfully arranged after the first frost.

Spinach

Spinach is a hardy, quick-growing vegetable that prefers cool weather. Seeds can be planted as soon as the ground can be worked, or in the late summer for a fall harvest. The plants mature in seven to eight weeks. Some gardeners have had success planting seeds as late as October in order to harvest a crop early the next spring. A thick mulch of leaves, straw, or (preferably) hay, is necessary to protect the plants through the winter. (In regions having severe winters, I doubt whether many of the plants would survive.)

Spade compost or well-rotted manure into the ground where you intend to plant the spinach. Plant the seeds at a depth of one-half inch, and cover them with a mixture of compost and soil. The seeds are slow to sprout, so I suggest you plant radishes among the spinach. The radishes will appear quickly, and identify the rows for you. After the seedlings appear, they should be thinned until they are two to three inches apart. Rows should be spaced at intervals of one to one-and-one-half feet.

Spinach is unique; the more rapidly it grows, the more tender its leaves are. Applications of fertilizer (a nitrate is probably best) and regular waterings encourage growth. Keep the soil loose by frequent cultivation. Though not necessary, a light mulch may help to reduce weeds and retain moisture in the soil around the plants.

There are two methods of harvesting. One involves removing the outer leaves; this permits the center sprouts to keep on producing new leaves. The other method is to harvest the entire plant, severing it at the stem close to the ground.

"New Zealand" spinach is a green, but it isn't spinach. It does taste like spinach, though, and can be used the same way — cooked, or served raw on a salad. It offers a certain advantage over spinach, since it can be grown in hot weather, and can survive heat that would wither spinach plants. It is larger than spinach, so its rows should be three feet apart, and the plants should be thinned to allow a distance of a foot between them. It matures in six weeks. Harvest it by removing the outer leaves. New leaves will grow to replace them, and the plant will continue producing for some time.

The spinach aphid is the only pest that poses a serious threat to your crop. It is very small, has a yellow or green body, and is generally found clustering on stems or beneath leaves. A light dusting of Rotenone should be sufficient to remove it. (For further remedies, refer to chapter 9).

Spinach blight is a virus that causes leaves to become yellow or blotched. Infected plants will cease growing and die. Disease resistant varieties of spinach are available. Your county agricultural agent or agricultural extension service can advise you as to which are the best varieties to plant in your area, and will tell you as well whether you need a disease-resistant strain.

Squash

Squash is a large plant, and gives a prolific yield. It is available in varieties suited for either warm or cool weather plantings.

Summer squash should not be planted until the soil has thoroughly warmed. Both summer and winter varieties can be placed in one-inch deep depressions

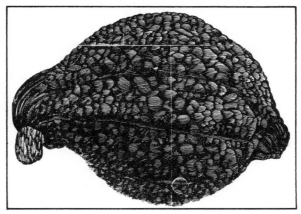

Winter squash is generally planted in late summer and harvested in the fall. Its fruit grows much larger than that of summer varieties. Summer squash can be eaten, skin, seeds, and all. Winter squash has a skin that is hard and inedible. Its seeds and pulp must be scooped out before it is baked. The seeds, however, may be saved, dried, and roasted.

Summer squash should not be planted until the soil has thoroughly warmed. Both summer and winter varieties can be placed in one inch deep depressions within a small mound of soil. Drop in three to five seeds. Hills of summer varieties should be planted at intervals of five feet. Hills of winter squash should be seven feet apart. Summer squash can also be planted in rows, an inch deep and ten inches apart. If you make use of hills, thin after the seedlings appear, leaving the two healthiest in each mound.

Squash must be watered heavily and frequently. A mulch placed around the mounds will help retain moisture and keep down weeds. These plants grow rapidly, and require plenty of nutrients. You can treat the soil before you sow the seeds. Or you can give the plants several feedings after they sprout. Use a liquid fertilizer, so the nutrients will become available to the plants more rapidly. Treating the soil with compost and other organic materials will also improve its ability to retain water.

The squash vine borer can be a very destructive pest. It seems especially active west of the Rockies. If you discover signs of insect activity, remove any badly wilted leaves, and pick off any bugs that you find. The borer can be controlled with applications of Malathion. Winter squash has less trouble with insects, because cool weather either kills the bugs or drives them into hiding.

Summer squash should be picked before the skin hardens. The fruit can be picked after it has reached a length of four inches, and before it grows over eight inches in length. Probe the skin with your fingernail; if it gives, the fruit is ready for harvest. To increase a plant's production of fruit, pick frequently.

Winter squash is harvested in late fall, after the skin has grown rather thick. When probed with your fingernail, the skin on a mature fruit should not give way. The stems on a winter bush are thick, so use a sharp knife to sever the stem two inches below the fruit. If the weather is sunny, leave the fruit out for several days, placing it on sheets of newspaper or burlap. This will allow it to harden, and is advisable if you intend to store the fruit for any length of time. Handle the squash carefully; even small bruises will cause the fruit to develop a rot. They will store best in a room with a temperature no higher than 60°.

Tomatoes

Every home garden I've ever seen has had them. Tomatoes have to be among the three or four most popular vegetables grown in this country. This is probably because few crops are easier to grow.

Tomatoes take from fifty to ninety days to mature and must, therefore, in all but the most temperate areas, be started indoors or purchased as seedlings. If you grow the plants from seed, start them at least six weeks before the projected date of the last frost. Start the seeds in a shallow pan. When the seedlings are at least three inches high, transplant them to a larger, deeper container. When you transplant them, pluck off all but the topmost leaves, and cover all but the upper third of the seedling with soil. This will force additional roots to form, giving the young plant strength. When the seedlings are nine to ten inches high, transplant them again following the same procedure as before. When it comes time to move the plants outdoors, they will have a well developed system of roots, capable of drawing in the amounts of nutrients the plants will require. Start hardening the plants off about a week before you move them outdoors.

Tomatoes seem to do best in a well-drained, very sunny location. They prefer a light, porous soil, so if you believe the spot you have selected has soil that is too heavy and dense, work in a large load of compost, and turn the ground thoroughly. Then work a dressing of a complete fertilizer and a load of well-rotted manure into the ground. The sun can dry out a seedling in less than a day, so it's a good idea to transplant the seedlings on a cloudy day. By their second or third day outdoors, they will have adapted to the summer sun.

Set the plants in deeply, burying as much as half to three quarters of the plant below ground. More roots will form along the buried section, and make an already strong plant ever stronger. A paper collar loosely fixed around the stem, and running an inch below ground and an inch above, will protect the seedlings from cutworm attacks. Leave a slight depression around the stem, to catch moisture for the plant. Water the ground frequently during the first month after transplanting. Once fruit begins to appear, you may reduce the frequency of these waterings. But should a lengthy dry spell occur, resume watering the rows regularly. The plants seem to benefit from a regular series of waterings — as opposed to random waterings, done whenever it occurs to you to do so. Throughout the life of the plant, try to maintain a steady, unvarying schedule of waterings. Even if you need to water them only once a week, try to do it on the same day every week.

You can save space in the garden by supporting the plants on stakes. Unstaked vines will sprawl across many valuable feet of the garden, and fruit touching the ground is more likely to develop rot or discoloration. Use stakes that are at least five feet high. Plant the seedlings about a foot from each stake, and between two to four feet apart. Each plant should be on the downwind side of a stake; that way, in a strong wind the plants will be blown against, and not away from, the stake. Otherwise, a plant could be damaged, or a part of it torn off. As the plant grows, you will have to tie it to the stake. Strips of cloth are firm, and have the advantage of not being sharp. There is no chance that they could bruise or cut the vine.

Only after the plants have been in the ground for a month, should you apply a dressing of mulch around the vines. Mulch tends to lower the temperature of the soil it covers, by blocking out the sun — and for at least their first month in the ground, tomato plants need soil as warm as the sun can make it.

When a plant reaches the top of its stake, pick the end of the vine off, to prevent it from growing further. To encourage the development of fruit, keep the vines free of suckers. Suckers are the tiny stems and leaves that appear in the crotches of the larger stems. They deprive a plant of the nourishment it requires to set fruit. I happen to think that staking tomato plants is a good idea, but many gardeners allow the vines to develop along the ground. If you decide to do that, plant the seedlings at least four feet apart, and spread a layer of clean straw or mulch beneath each plant (this will serve to protect the fruit from damage).

Tomatoes are ready for harvesting when they are large, firm, and uniform in color. Large green tomatoes can be removed at the end of the season. They will ripen in several weeks; wrap each in newspaper and store them in a place that is cool, humid and dark. To remove the fruit from a plant, simply grasp it and give it a gentle tug.

Few pests seriously affect a tomato plant. The bizarre tomato hornworm looks a good deal more dangerous than it is. If you find any on the leaves of a plant, lift them off and destroy them. Tomatoes are unfortunately susceptible to a variety of diseases. The best remedy for such trouble is to buy seed varieties that have been treated in order to be disease resistant. Your county agricultural agent should be able to recommend several disease resistant varieties that do well in your area. Some chemicals can be used to treat diseases, but it is probably a better, and less expensive, idea to pull out and discard any badly infected vines.

Some gardeners encourage early bearing on their vines by adding several loads of compost to the soil before they bring their tomato plants outdoors. They then strip all but the topmost leaves from each seedling, and place all but the top three inches of the plant below the ground. Around each plant, they apply a heavy dressing of mulch. It is said that such a method (a more radical version of the aforementioned method of encouraging roots) can bring plants to maturity by the middle of July.

Turnips

Turnips are a hardy, cool weather crop that can be grown in almost any sort of climate. They can be planted in early spring or, as is frequently done, in late summer. Turnip varieties produce crops in a number of sizes and shapes, and all require between forty-five to sixty days to mature.

Turnips taste best when they grow rapidly, and a well prepared soil will quicken the rate of growth. Work the soil, to make it loose and friable. Mix in a dressing of a complete fertilizer and organic material. This step is also important because turnips are frequently planted in a spot previously occupied by some other, midsummer crop. The soil will probably need replenishing, so be sure to give it an ample dressing.

Plant the seeds in a shallow furrow, covering them with a quarter-inch of soil, or with a mixture of soil, sand, and peat moss in equal parts. This soil mixture is said to encourage successful germination, but it is not absolutely necessary. Rows should be spaced twelve to fifteen inches apart. Keep the soil loose and free of weeds, by cultivating shallowly , and don't weed at all until you have identified the turnip seedlings. Spreading a mulch around the plants will provide nutrients and discourage weeds. When the seedlings are four to five inches tall, thin the rows until there is a space of five or six inches between plants. During dry weather, water two or three times a week.

When the tops of the plants are three to four inches in diameter, pull the turnips out. If allowed to remain in the ground too long, they will become bitter and coarse. You can store turnips by removing their tops, and storing the bulbs in boxes filled with clean sand or sawdust. They seem to remain fresh for long periods if kept in an area having a temperature of less than forty degrees.

Most gardeners prefer to use only the root of the plant, but its leaves can also be used in a variety of dishes.

Aphids may settle on turnip leaves. They can usually be discouraged by directing a strong stream of water onto the leaves — but do so only after you are convinced of their presence. Cabbage loopers may also occasionally attack turnips, but an application of Malathion should be all you need to control them. Don't apply any chemicals to the crop within two weeks of your projected harvest date.

Chapter   Four

CONTAINER GARDENING

You don't need an outside garden in order to raise vegetables. If you live in an apartment, or just in the city, you probably won't have access to much, if any, ground. But you can still raise a variety of crops, every bit as large and healthy as those produced in some spacious suburban plot. All you need is soil, and something to put the soil in. Many kinds of vegetables can be successfully grown in containers placed on a sunny windowsill, a terrace, or even on a roof.

Artichokes, beets, broccoli, cabbage, cauliflower, chard, eggplant, lettuce, peppers, radishes, spinach, and tomatoes are among the vegetables that adapt without difficulty to containers. Many vegetables — corn, for example — that in their full-grown state would prove unwieldy in a container, are now available in miniature varieties. These newly developed plants are smaller than those grown in the garden, but will yield almost as much as a full sized plant.

Gardening in containers has often been presented as a last resort for those without land. The suggestion seems to be that it is somehow inferior to gardening outdoors. In fact, I believe that in several ways container gardens are superior. Weeding is obviously an occasional, light task. Moreover, when you raise vegetables in containers, your growing season is twelve months long. So even if you tend a sizable garden through the summer, you may want to keep several plants in containers, to supply yourself with a favorite vegetable through the fall and winter. In the depth of winter, few things are more pleasant than picking ripe vegetables for your supper.

Vegetables have the same requirements no matter where they are grown. They need plenty of sunlight. They need water. And they need food. Before you buy seeds or containers, sit down and decide what varieties you want to grow. Then take a long look at your rooms. How many sunny windows do you have? Windows having a southern or eastern exposure are those best for your plants. Windows with a western or northern exposure are not suitable because they receive little direct sunlight. You can supplement sunlight with a battery of fluorescent lamps (see Supplies for a list of manufacturers), but you will have to accept higher electric bills. Just as in the garden, plants cannot be jammed together on a windowsill or under artificial light without causing damage. So be quite specific in deciding just how many containers you can fit into your rooms. Then, draw up a list of the number and size of the containers you need.

If you can't afford to spend much money on containers, don't worry. Vegetables can be grown in almost anything having a bottom and sides. I've heard of gardeners using clay and plastic pots, buckets, baskets, boxes, milk crates, and garbage pails to raise a crop. Whatever you use, it should be capable of holding at least six, and preferably eight to twelve, inches of soil. A large container, such as a tub or barrel, can provide space for several plants, but once filled with soil it may prove impossible to move. So if you intend to use large containers, select for them a spot where they can remain undisturbed.

If windowsill or terrace space is at a premium, as it usually is, hang your plants up. Use a clay pot, or a hanging basket provided with drainage holes. Filled with soil, such containers are heavy, so use a large hook placed securely in a wall or ceiling, and double the wire supports.

Before you use any container, even if you've just brought it home from the store, wash it in hot soapy water and rinse it thoroughly with cold water.

Excess water must have a means of escape. If the soil remains constantly moist, it will encourage the growth of molds, diseases, and rots. If the containers you're using have no drainage holes, drill several on either side close to, but not on, the bottom. Unless the containers are small enough to be placed on saucers (available, along with clay or plastic pots, from garden centers), you will have to provide some alternative means for catching the run-off, such as a sheet of plastic spread under the containers. There won't be much water running out of the drainage holes, but there will be some, and you should be prepared for it.

You'll need soil. It should be light and loose, not compacted. A number of sterile soil mixes are available from mail order garden supply firms and from garden supply centers. Such mixes generally include a dose of fertilizer, and are guaranteed to be free of disease-producing organisms. You can spade up soil from a park, but it would probably be too heavy and compacted (to say nothing of illegal), and would have to be greatly diluted in order to be used; it would certainly contain disease spores and insect eggs. Although some expense is involved in purchasing sufficient soil for your containers, I advise you to do so. If you need to economize, you can buy large bags of the necessary soil ingredients for slightly less than a prepared mix, and can combine them yourself. The most frequently cited formula calls for one part garden loam, one part peat moss — both are materials that should be readily available at a garden center. Before you pour the mix into your containers, cover the drainage holes with pieces of broken crockery. Position the shards so that they cover — but do not block — the drainage holes. Or you can cover the bottom of the container with an inch of clean gravel or perlite (available at garden centers). Such coarse materials serve to slow, but not stop, the flow of water. If the drainage holes are rather large, you'll have to line the bottom of the container with wire mesh, to prevent the coarse material from being carried out with the water.

You can purchase seedlings from a garden center or greenhouse, or else raise plants from seed. If you plant seeds, start them in flats or other large, shallow containers. When the seedlings are two to three inches high, you can transplant them to their permanent containers. If you intend to move them outdoors onto a terrace or roof, or into a small backyard, they will have to be "hardened off." About two weeks before you plan to leave them out, begin setting them outdoors for several hours each day. Gradually increase the amount of time they spend outdoors, until they are outside the entire day. Hardening a plant off prepares it, by toughening it, to withstand chill winds and variable temperatures without going into trauma. If a plant stops growing for more than a week after you have set it out, or if most of its foliage wilts, it is in trauma. Carry it back indoors, water it, and enclose both container and plant in a plastic bag. Close the bag, and allow the plant to remain inside for several days. If the plant improves, begin hardening it off again.

Give the plants frequent small waterings. Whenever you water, some moisture should be running out of the drainage holes. Water a plant until the surface is everywhere moist to the touch, but not waterlogged. Soil that has become waterlogged will turn thick and sticky, and may be compacted into a suffocating mass around the roots. If you're growing plants in small containers, you can immerse them, to a point just below the rim of the pot, in a tub of lukewarm water. Stand them in the tub, and leave them there until beads of moisture appear on the surface of the soil. Always water in the morning, so your plants will have moisture to draw on throughout the day. Don't water in the evening — plants need much less water at night.

Give the plants a diluted dose of a "complete" fertilizer once every other week. You can mix it in with their water. Some gardeners apply a mulch to the surface of their container plants, but I don't think the practice is either necessary or wise. Mulching a garden is often recommended because so many factors, such as light

and moisture, cannot be controlled; mulching allows you to exert some control. Mulch is a term used to describe any organic material applied in a layer around crops, to conserve moisture, maintain an even soil temperature and control weeds.
But when you grow vegetables in containers, you really can control almost every aspect of their development. It's much easier to give them sufficient water and food. Insects are not a major problem (mulching is said to discourage some pests). You can move them into and out of sunlight as you think necessary. And weeding is a minor task. If you apply mulch to your containers, you may be causing yourself avoidable problems.

So I don't think mulching is a good idea, but I do think applying occasional dressings of compost is an excellent practice. You can start a compost heap in a garbage can. Not only will you produce excellent food for your plants, you'll be recycling garbage that would otherwise be added to some noisome dump.

If you keep plants on the roof of your building, you'll have to keep a layer of material between the containers and the surface of the roof. You can set the plants on several layers of newspaper, or on a layer of canvas. During midsummer, the heat reflected by the surface of the roof could otherwise scorch the containers and the plant's tender roots. However, during late summer and early fall this will work to your favor: the additional heat given off by the surface will extend your growing season by up to several weeks. If you do set containers out on the roof, don't use large, heavy containers. Reserve them for a terrace.

If you live in an urban area, but have a small backyard, you can of course grow some vegetables there. But the soil will probably need some work before you can plant anything. Remember that much of the ground now exposed in a city was once covered by structures since torn down. The soil may be hard and badly compacted. There may be refuse close to the surface. I remember one gardener who began enthusiastically spading up a lot, and discovered several inches below the surface an asphalt driveway, still intact! He didn't get his garden.

Spade up the soil and work it thoroughly. Mix in fertilizer and manure. A load of peat moss will help to lighten the soil. Plant only in those parts of the yard that receive at least six hours of sunlight a day. You can increase the size of your garden by making use of fences or walls for climbing crops. And, although you are gardening outdoors, you should encounter less trouble with insects or disease than gardeners in the suburbs or country. Of course, there are exceptions to any rule. Some insects are bound to find their way to your garden, and you will have to deal with them. The care of a city garden does not differ from the care required of a garden in the suburbs. You must be diligent in watering, feeding and weeding. Whether you're gardening in a bucket or a backyard, the basics remain the same.

Chapter  Five

THE SOIL

The quality of the soil in which you sow your seeds has a greater effect on the outcome of your garden than any other feature. Poor soil, low in nutrients or incapable of absorbing or holding moisture, will produce stunted crops, or no crops at all. Good soil consistently produces large crops. What makes a "good" soil?

The ability to soak up water quickly.

Good drainage, allowing the water to rapidly pass through.

The ability to remain loose and crumbly in texture.

A structure that is loose enough to allow air to readily penetrate.

The soil is a storehouse of all the elements your plants need to survive and grow. If it is deficient in some way, incapable of absorbing or retaining moisture, nutrients or air, your crops will have a hard time of it. However, problems with soil need never prove fatal to your plans for a productive garden. Even the most unpromising soil can be brought into excellent condition in the space of two seasons.

The primary elements of any topsoil are sand, clay and humus. Sand contributes to good drainage. If your soil has an insufficient supply of sand, it will probably tend to become waterlogged. Too much sand in a soil, and water will pass through it so rapidly that plants will not have a chance to draw upon it. Sand is easy to work. It warms up early in the spring. But, by itself, it is an unsatisfactory material for growing vegetables. Quantities of coarse organic materials, such as compost, well rotted manure and peat moss, will improve the texture of a sandly soil, making it ideal for vegetable gardening.

Clay absorbs water slowly and retains it for lengthy periods. It stores nutrients for a lengthier period than any other element. A soil with a high percentage of clay can form a hard surface when the weather is hot and dry, making it hard to work.

After rain, clay becomes lumpy. In either condition, it will obstruct the development of growing plants, if it does not kill them. Organic materials, such as compost or peat moss, greatly improve the structure of a soil with too much clay. It will accept water without becoming waterlogged, and air will be able to freely penetrate the ground.

Few areas have soil with large amounts of humus. Wherever it is present, humus is of great benefit to a soil. It is composed of decayed organic materials, such as plants and leaves. Thus, it is especially rich in nutrients. It can be of value to any garden, as it also stores water and makes it easier for air to pass through the soil.

Most gardener's aren't fortunate enough to start off with a good, balanced soil. It has to be developed. However, you can turn even the most unpromising of soils into good soil in the space of two growing seasons.

You can begin work on improving a poor soil as soon as the ground is warm enough to work. Spade in quantities of organic materials. Break the material up and work it well into the top six to eight inches of soil. This method is often referred to as "sheet composting". It's a good idea to apply sheet compost again in the fall, after all the crops have been gathered in. There will be quite a lot of organic waste laying about in your garden after the vegetables have been removed. Rather than raking it up to be carted away, mix it with peat moss or manure and spade the mix into the ground.

You might also want to sow a "green manure" crop in late summer or early fall. Clover, rye, soybeans, oats, buckwheat and vetch are all excellent cover crops. They protect the soil from the harsh effects of the winter, add nitrogen to the soil, and can be turned into the soil in the spring, as part of your soil improvement program.

A compost pile should be an important part of your soil improvement program. If you have a vegetable garden, I think you should have a compost pile. Composting is actually a method of speeding up the processes of nature. The remains of leaves, grasses and animals on uncultivated land are normally worked on by microorganisms and the elements, until they are reduced to components that can be absorbed by the soil.

A compost heap accelerates this process. The result of the process, in nature or in a compost pile, is a nutrient rich humus ideally suited for use in a garden. One of the most attractive features of the practice is its utilization of materials that would otherwise go to waste, such as leaves, grass clippings and garbage.

The idea is to combine a variety of ingredients in such a way that soil bacteria will proliferate, and act to rapidly break the materials down into their organic components. If the bacteria are to accomplish this task, they need moisture, air and food.

70

To give the bacteria the conditions they need, materials should be gathered into a pile. While compost can be made in an open pile, a container of some sort will keep the process well organized. Unless you have a very large garden, a pile covering a four by six foot area should be all you need.

You begin the pile by spreading a layer of waste material over the area marked off for the pile, or in the container. Leaves, grass clippings, plants, vines, straw, hay, sawdust, weeds, coffee grounds, wood ashes, and other kitchen refuse can all be used. Any large materials, such as leaves, vines or plants pulled from the garden after the vegetables have been removed, should be chopped or shredded before being added to the pile. Large surfaces tend to slow the process down.

The first layer of organic material should be six to eight inches thick. The next layer should be composed of topsoil and manure, with two cupfuls of a fertilizer (such as blood meal) mixed in. The manure and fertilizer are sources of food for the bacteria. Moisten this layer thoroughly, to encourage an even distribution of fertilizer. The third layer should again be one of organic materials, and the fourth should be the soil-manure mix. Keep alternating the layers until the pile is four to five feet high, or until you have exhausted your supply of materials. Scoop out a basin in the middle of the top layer, to simplify watering and provide a basin for collecting rain.

Keep the pile moist — but not soggy. During hot, dry weather this may mean watering the pile every three or four days. During periods of prolonged rainfall, cover the pile with a sheet of plastic.

Turn the pile every two to three weeks. This encourages the air circulation so essential to the proliferation of bacteria. It also discourages odors. When you turn the pile, the outer materials, least affected by the process of decomposistion going on in the middle of the pile, are moved towards the center, so that they in turn will be broken down.

The compost will be ready to use in as little as three months, or as long as five. When you can no longer identify any of the components of the mix, your compost is ready. If all of the material is put through a shredder before being added to the pile, the compost may be ready in as little time as a month. Smaller pieces decompose more rapidly. Shredded material makes a light, fluffy mix, which facilitates the easy passage of air and water throughout the pile.

Many gardeners start their pile in the fall, to have it ready for use in the spring. If you build a pile in warm weather, it will have to be turned more frequently. Some gardeners maintain two piles — one begun the previous fall, the other started in the spring — so that they will be assured of a sufficient supply of compost throughout the spring and summer.

Compost is inexpensive and easy to make and maintain, yet it is extraordinarily valuable stuff. Whether you intend to use it to improve the soil or feed your crops, compost is an essential part of good gardening.

Gardening in Raised Beds

If your soil is hard to work and slow to drain, you will have to put considerable effort into improving it. If you would prefer not to expend the time and money required to bring a poor soil into prime condition, you can grow vegetables in raised beds. You make a raised bed by standing two-by-twelve inch redwood boards on the surface of the ground. The boards should run parallel, and should be spaced four to five feet apart. The rectangular beds should be reinforced at the corners. Stakes should be nailed at intervals along the outer surface of the boards, and driven into the soil. Fill the beds with a rich soil mix, including such materials as compost, manure, peat moss and fertilizer, along with topsoil. Before sowing seeds in the beds, soak the soil mix, so that it will settle. If you postpone watering until after dropping the seeds in place, the soil will settle and take the seeds with it. Water the soil as you would in a regular garden. A dose of fertilizer, midway through the growing season, may be necessary.

It's easier to control pests within the well defined structure of a bed. In fact, it's somewhat easier to do everything. You don't have to do so much bending to weed and water the crops. The soil in the beds tends to warm earlier in the spring, meaning that you can plant earlier. If frost threatens, you can cover each bed with a sheet of plastic.

French Intensive Gardening

This method, developed centuries ago by European farmers, has been used with great success to produce large yields from unpromising soils. It calls for closely spaced raised beds, treated with quantities of organic materials. The materials, thoroughly mixed into the soil, improve its consistency, and make further applications of fertilizer unnecessary. The raised beds are said to improve aeration and promote good drainage. However, the technique requires hard, back-straining labor, for the entire area of the garden must be dug out, and the soil and amendments thoroughly mixed and spaded back in place. If the soil in your plot is heavy and hard to work, this method might be what you need to turn an unpromising location into a successful garden. Otherwise, intensive gardening is, in my opinion, more work than it is worth.

To work your soil in the French intensive manner, you must first cover the entire garden surface with a one to two inch layer of compost, well rotted manure, fertilizer and any other materials you wish to add. Beginning at one end of the plot, dig down two shovels full. Set the soil aside. Dig down again. Mix the compost and other amendments into the excavated soil, then shovel it into the hole you first shoveled out. Repeat this procedure throughout the garden, digging two trenches at a time, and using the soil, mixed with materials, to refill the holes. You can finish by filling the last hole with soil dug from the point where you began. If you do not wish to treat the entire garden in this manner, you can mark out beds three to four feet wide, and treat only these areas. When you are finished, the ground will be slightly mounded. Let the beds sit for several days, then rake them until the soil is loose and without clots. A final light dressing of manure, wood ashes bone meal or rock phosphate can be mixed into the top four inches a day before you intend to plant. Water the ground, using a light spray rather than a forceful stream to thoroughly wet the soil.

Seeds should be applied liberally to the treated areas. The seedlings should be thinned until the leaves of the young plants touch, but do not overlap. Leaf and root crops do well in such situations. Most plants producing fruit do not.

You may want to experiment with this method, by creating a small bed so that you can match the size of its yield with the crops harvested from a single or wide row. Unless you have particularly heavy soil, that is close to unworkable, I can't recommend this method. It does pay off, but only after many hours of hard work.

Chapter  Six

SOWING

Vegetable crops cannot be planted outdoors until all danger of frost has passed and the soil has been warmed by the summer sun. By starting such crops indoors, in flats, six to eight weeks before they could be started outdoors, you can greatly extend your growing season. When the plants can finally be moved outdoors, they will already be well developed, hardy seedlings. Starting plants indoors also helps you avoid hazards — among them, birds, heavy rain, unexpected cold fronts, and weeds — that frequently prove fatal to seedlings. It is also an excellent way to introduce your children to the basics of plant growth and gardening.

To raise a large crop of healthy seedlings you will need containers, a disease-free growing medium, a steady supply of light, warmth, and moisture to insure successful germination and growth, and some fertilizer. Broccoli, cabbage, cauliflower, celery, eggplant, lettuce, onions, peppers, and tomatoes all benefit from being started indoors. Hardy, cool season crops need not be started inside, as conditions in the garden in early spring do not affect them.

Tomato, eggplant, and pepper seeds should be started six to eight weeks before you anticipate being able to move them outdoors. Broccoli, cabbage, and cauliflower should be planted only four to five weeks before they can be moved outdoors. Begun any earlier, they would grow so large as to be unwieldy. Don't plant any seeds more than eight weeks before they can be transplanted outside: they would grow too large to be easily handled, and their need for nutrients and sunlight might be more than you could provide.

You can sow seeds in almost any size or shape of container, so long as it provides for the drainage of excess water, and is not so large as to be cumbersome to move about. Wooden flats, two feet long, a foot wide, and five to six inches deep, make excellent containers for seedlings. The bottom of such a flat should be a series of slats, spaced a quarter of an inch apart, to allow for proper drainage. Because you can sow more seeds in a flat than in most other containers, flats simplify the care of the seedlings: it's much easier to tend one large container than a number of small ones.

You can fill the containers with sterilized soil, soil mixes, or vermiculite. If you are using soil, don't just shovel it out of your garden. Your soil may be of excellent quality, but it is certain to contain weed seeds, and may well conceal insect eggs and disease organisms, any of which could prove fatal to your seedlings. You can sterilize the soil by baking it in your oven for an hour at a temperature of 375 degrees, or you can treat it with formaldehyde. Both processes are difficult and noisome. Unless you need a quantity of soil, I suggest that you purchase a soil mix at a garden center. Such mixes as Jiffy Mix, Redi-Earth, and Pro-Mix are sterilized and contain all the nutrients your seedlings will need. If you want to make your own soil mix, you can buy the ingredients and combine them yourself. Vermiculite, a light-weight expanded mica, can be used separately as a soil medium, or it can be used as part of a soil mix. Your home-made mix should include four quarts of vermiculite, four quarts of shredded peat moss, two tablespoons of ground limestone, and three tablespoons of a 5-10-5 fertilizer. A simpler, but equally effective formula calls for one quart of vermiculite, one quart of garden loam, and one quart of peat moss. These proportions can be adapted to the quantity you desire.

Peat pellets are compressed tablets of peat moss, already treated with fertilizer. Placed in water, a pellet expands into a two inch container. A single seed is then tucked into the surface of it. Pellets are available under such brand names as Jiffy-7, BR8 Blocks, and Kys-Kubes.

Pots are available composed entirely of peat moss or some other fibrous organic material. Both pellets and pots are very absorbent and quick to drain, and both include nutrients. Their most attractive feature is that they can be set into the ground. A seedling need not be removed from its container; its roots are thus spared disturbance and the chance of injury. Once in the ground such containers will gradually dissolve, providing a steady supply of nutrients to the seedlings. The only drawback to the use of pots or pellets is that only one seed can be placed in each. Purchasing enough containers to start a crop can therefore prove quite expensive. Moreover, a number of small containers takes up more space than just a large flat.

If you choose to sow seeds in a flat or other large container, first cover the bottom with wire mesh, to prevent soil from being carried away with any excess water. If the container has several drainage holes, rather than intervals between slats, a quarter-inch of clean gravel will serve the same purpose. Pour in enough soil mix to reach half an inch below the rim of the container. Use the edge of a board or a ruler to level the mix.

Seeds can be planted in rows along the surface, or in parallel depressions. You can lay individual seeds in rows across the surface of the mix. Distribute them evenly, and not too thickly. Then cover them with a thin layer of soil, or vermiculite, or moistened peat moss. To plant them in depressions, use a round-stick or a pencil to make the rows, spacing them four inches apart. If planted on the surface, seeds should be in rows three inches apart. Scatter seeds thinly along the depressions. Go back and gently press the seeds into the bottom of each trench. Fill the depressions with soil, and level the surface.

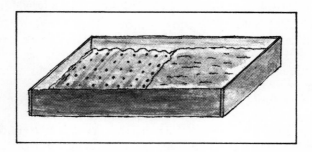

If you intend to plant seeds in containers filled with vermiculite, thoroughly water the material first. Then sow the seeds in rows, placing them in holes a quarter of an inch to half an inch deep. Put no more than one seed in each hole. Gently brush vermiculite over the seeds, until the surface is level. Cover the container with a sheet of paper, or enclose it in a plastic bag. This will serve to maintain a high level of moisture around the seeds, and so encourage successful germination. When the seedlings appear above the surface, remove the covering. As soon as second pairs of leaves appear on the seedlings, they should be transplanted into containers filled with a soil mix. One advantage of starting seeds in vermiculite is the ease with which they can be lifted out; this lessens the chance of doing damage to tender roots. Space the seedlings more widely apart in their second container. Plant them so that their leaves are about half an inch above the surface. Set the seedlings into depressions, gently brushing in soil until the holes are filled.

Peat pellets and pots must be thoroughly moistened before seeds are placed in them. After planting, the containers should be placed inside a plastic bag to prevent them from drying out. Remove them as soon as the seedlings appear. From the start, place what you plant in the warmest location in your house — no matter what they are planted in. Plants need warmth, not light, in order to germinate.

After planting, flats can be covered with a sheet of glass: this serves the same purpose plastic bags do for smaller containers. Spread sheets of newspaper across the surface of the glass. Generally, this is helpful, but it is less necessary with large containers than with small pots. As long as the soil has been thoroughly watered before planting, the seeds should germinate without difficulty.

Seedlings need as much sunlight as possible. Place your containers in windows having southern or eastern exposures. Turn the flats and pots every other day, to prevent the plants from leaning continuously toward light and growing up crooked. Position the containers so that they do not block each other from the light. On cold nights, move the flats or pots away from the glass. You might even do well to remove them from the window at night and put them back in the morning.

If your rooms don't receive at least six hours of direct sunlight daily, you will need fluorescent lamps to supplement, or entirely replace, the sun. Several units are available that have been especially designed for use with plants. Their tubes concentrate more energy in the red, far red and blue areas of the spectrum — light rays essential for proper plant growth. Such units are not inexpensive, and you should consider carefully whether the purchase is necessary. If you're starting a good many plants indoors, you probably won't have enough window sills to do the job, and so will need some other light source.

To sprout seeds, position containers four inches below the tubes. Keep the unit on until seedlings emerge. Once the seedlings have appeared, keep the unit running for just twelve hours a day. Place the flats or other containers a foot below the tubes.

As soon as a seedling produces its second pair of leaves, it should be transplanted into a deeper container. Transplanting a seedling gives it the additional space it requires to continue growing, and it encourages the development of a strong root system.

Water the flat or pots before you remove the seedlings; this will make soil adhere to, and thus protect, the plant's tender roots. You can use a hand trowel to carefully loosen the soil around each seedling. Gently grasp one of the leaves, and slowly lift the seedlings out, one at a time. Try not to touch the stem of a plant — it is quite fragile — and never, on any account, touch the roots. The seedlings should be replanted to have at least an inch of space on every side. If they grow so quickly that they must be transplanted again, plant them at intervals of three inches.

Dissolve a small dose of a complete fertilizer in water, and apply it to the soil as soon as the seedlings have been set in place. After that, thoroughly water the containers once every other day, using a fine spray. Use lukewarm water. Unless the seedlings are transplanted again, they should be given only one more weak dose of fertilizer.

Hardening-Off Seedlings

If young plants are moved directly from a protected environment into the garden, they are likely to go into shock, fail to resume growth, wilt, and perhaps even die. You must prepare seedlings for such a transition by exposing them to outdoor conditions gradually.

You can begin by placing them on the sill of an open window. On the first afternoon, leave the window open for just a half hour. Over the space of a week, increase the amount of time the window remains open, until the plants are spending the entire afternoon there. Start about three weeks before you intend to transplant the seedlings into the garden. After a week of such limited exposure, the plants should be ready for their first trip outdoors. Carry the containers outside, and position them in partial shade. Leave them out for several hours, beginning in late morning or early afternoon. After two to three days, the containers can be moved into full sunlight. As the weather warms, and as the plants become increasingly adjusted to their environment, they can be left out for longer and longer periods. Bring them in before evening, and don't leave them out through a prolonged rain. Keep the containers in a location that is well sheltered from the wind: strong chilly winds can throw them into shock, and even snap the stems of particularly tender plants.

Transplanting

By the end of the third week, the seedlings should be sufficiently hardened to adapt without difficulty to their life outdoors. By now, all danger of frost should be past, and the ground should be malleable enough to work. You can now transplant the seedlings.

Begin preparing the garden several days before you intend to set the plants in place. Turn the soil, and thoroughly mix fertilizer and organic materials into it. (For specific instructions on preparing the soil, see Chapter 5.) Lay out the rows, and dig holes for the plants. Then wait for a cloudy day.

By now the seedlings will have been toughened considerably, but they will still experience an initial shock when transplanted. Intense sunlight and high temperatures can only complicate the condition. So wait for a cloudy day. If it continues sunny and very warm, however, you may have to fashion some protection for the plants. In either case, within a day, they should be adjusted to their new environment.

Bring the containers outside. Fill each of the holes in the ground with water, and let the water soak in. Water the containers thoroughly too; this will encourage soil to cling to the roots and protect them from bruising or the drying effect of the air, and will make the removal of the plants easier. Use your fingers or a spoon to gently lift each seedling out of its container.

If the seedlings have been grown in peat pots, blocks, or cubes, water the entire container thoroughly, and place it in a hole. Brush soil around and on top of the container, until it is entirely covered. It will soon begin to dissolve, releasing nutrients into the soil. Level the ground around the plants, so that there are no mounds to deflect water.

Seedlings removed from containers should be lowered carefully into the holes prepared for them. Cover the roots with loose soil, brushing it down around them. Continue to brush soil into a depression until it is filled. Then, level the soil around each plant. Next, tug at the tip of a leaf on each of the transplanted seedlings. If the plant moves noticeably towards you, inclining its entire stem, it is not firmly enough in place. To survive and grow properly, and to resist strong winds, a plant must be held tightly in the soil, so firm the ground around the plant. Finally, give all of the plants a lengthy watering. This will encourage the soil to settle around the roots. Fill in any depressions that appear around the plants after watering. A strong dose of a phosphate fertilizer, applied with the water, will encourage rapid, healthy root formation. If you have not yet planted any seeds in the garden, a watering can may be all that is required for this initial watering. If you use a hose, attach a nozzle with a fine spray adjustment. Water the ground, not the plants. Plants draw in water through their roots, not their leaves.

This procedure applies both to any seedlings you may have raised and to seedlings you have purchased. There is, however, one difference. Before transplanting purchased seedlings, check them thoroughly for signs of insects. Bugs can find their way into a garden fast enough without getting a helping hand. Remove individual bugs, and if a seedling seems badly infested, discard it.

Cutworms —long, plump worms — can play havoc with a row of young plants. Emerging at night to feed, they will wrap themselves around, and chew partway

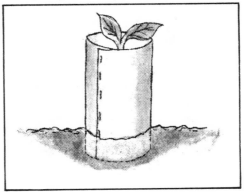

through, the stems of tender seedlings. Plants that have been attacked look as though they've been beheaded: most of the stem will have toppled over onto the ground. You can avoid such destruction by placing a cardboard or paper collar around the seedlings upon transplantation. The collar should extend about an inch below the soil, and two inches above it. It should clear the stem by at least half an inch all the way around. The worms will be unable to reach the seedlings. By the time the plants are strong enough to discourage attack (cutworms prefer seedlings, and rarely trouble larger plants), the collar will have largely dissolved. Remove any remaining pieces so that it will not interfere with the growth of the plant. You can fashion your own collars from cardboard, sheets of newspaper, or other paper, or aluminum foil, or you can purchase collars of tarred paper from some mail order houses, and at some garden centers.

Sowing Seeds Outdoors

Sowing seed directly into the garden gives you less control over the factors affecting germination, especially the quantities of warmth and light. Still, by not rushing the season, by thoroughly preparing the seedbed, by watering as required, and most importantly, by carefully following the sowing instructions printed on each seed packet, you can avoid most problems associated with sowing seeds outdoors.

When you sow depends on the weather and the kinds of crops you are planting: different crops have greatly differing abilities to withstand cold. Most root crops, and some leaf crops, won't rot if planted in cold soil. Some crops, identified in the Profiles, can even withstand a late frost without harm. But the seeds of most fruiting crops will rot if planted too early, and in soil that is still very cold. Your county agricultural agent will be able to suggest planting dates for some crops. An inexpensive soil thermometer, available at garden centers, will give you an accurate reading of the soil temperature. It is safe to sow most kinds of seeds when the thermometer indicates a steady temperature of sixty degrees, though it is better to wait until the temperature reaches sixty five degrees.

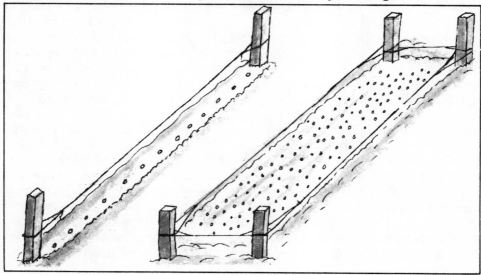

You can sow seeds in single or wide rows, depending on the crops involved and your preferences. In single row planting, seeds are placed in a single line down a straight row. Generally, seeds are simply dropped into a furrow or into individual holes. In a wide row, no excavations are made. A wide row is about a foot wide — three times the width of a single row. After establishing the boundaries of a wide row, seed is broadcast over the entire area. Then the surface of the row is covered with a layer of soil or organic materials, such as a mulch.

Because plants in a wide row grow so closely together, it is said that the frequency with which the area must be weeded is greatly reduced. In a reversal of the common situation, the seedlings deprive the weeds of light! Because all of the plants can be easily reached, it is said to be easier to cultivate the plants and harvest the crop. At any rate, a wide row will produce a larger harvest than a comparable length of single rows. But — not all crops are suited to wide-row planting. Beets, carrots, lettuce, peas, and snap beans are among those most likely to adapt successfully to such a design. Other crops do better planted in single rows.

Water the garden before you begin sowing the crops. Damp soil is easier to work than dry soil. If you are planting in single rows, use a corner of a hoe to draw long shallow parallel trenches across the garden. The rows should run from north to south. Only if you are gardening on a slope should the rows run from east to west; this is to prevent erosion. Drive in pegs at both ends of the furrow, and stretch tautly a length of twine between them. This will indicate if the furrows you've drawn are reasonably straight. Straight rows won't make the plants grow any faster, but will help you to identify seedlings and to spot and remove weeds. Moreover, a neat garden simply looks better than one arranged haphazardly.

You can drop seeds into the furrow, or make individual depressions for them. Gently brush soil over the seeds, until the furrow or holes have been filled in. Follow the depth estimates given on each seed packet. A seed planted too close to the surface may dry out and fail to germinate. A seed pushed too deep into the soil will die before its sprout can reach the surface. You can tap seeds from a packet onto the soil, or you can hold seeds in your palm, and drop them in place by rubbing each between the thumb and forefinger of your other hand.

Remove the pegs and twine after the rows have been planted. Water the rows with a light spray, and continue to water the plot daily until the seeds have sprouted. Don't apply a forceful stream of water to the garden; it can drive away soil, thereby exposing the seeds and perhaps even carrying them away. A perforated garden hose, producing an even, fine spray, is the best way to water a just-planted garden.

More seeds than are needed are always planted, to allow for those that don't germinate, and for those that don't survive the first month. Even with a moderate mortality rate, more seedlings than are needed will survive. Too many plants in a row will cause all of the plants to suffer, since they will deprive one another of vital sunlight and nutrients. Leaf crops in an overcrowded row will wilt, root crops will grow stunted or become distorted, and vine crops will give greatly reduced yields. It may seem like folly, but thin the rows several days after the sprouts appear above the surface. Pull the seedlings out by hand. Work your way down each row, thinning so that there is an equivalent amount of space around each remaining seedling. Thin again, one to two weeks later. Try to leave the healthiest looking seedlings in place. Thin the rows this time until there is between the plants the amount of space recommended in the Profiles. The thinnings of leaf crops, and of some root crops, can be eaten. Other thinnings can be added to your compost pile.

Wide rows should be thinned as soon as the plants are about a half an inch tall. You can use a rake to do the job, dragging it slowly across the surface of the row. Don't probe deeply into the soil, or you may damage the fragile roots of the plants. Thin repeatedly until the recommended distance between plants has been achieved.

One final reminder: sowing seeds and tending seedlings isn't difficult. Just follow the rules, work slowly, and work carefully.

Chapter  Seven

TENDING THE GARDEN

A well-tended garden is a healthy garden. And healthy plants are better able to withstand infections and insect attacks. In fact, the healthier the plant, the larger and more attractive its yield will be. You can keep your plants healthy by maintaining a weed-free garden, by watering the plot as it is required, and by applying nutrients to the soil.

You needn't spend hours toiling in your garden. Frequent, brief periods of work will usually be all that is required. But you must be diligent, and establish a regular schedule for inspecting the plot and doing whatever must be done. Every time you go into the garden, look for weeds. Immediately pull or hoe out any that you find. Water the garden as you think it is required, basing your judgment on the frequency of rain and the varying requirements of different crops. Several applications of fertilizer will be necessary, to provide the crops with nutrients essential for their health and continued growth. Remember too that it takes less time to do things right than to correct mistakes. So establish a regular schedule, and stick to it. If you're like most gardeners, you'll be out in your garden every day anyway, inspecting, watching, enjoying the appearance and the progress of the garden you've made.

Cultivation

The soil in your garden must be loose and weed-free. To keep it that way, you'll need a hoe, occasionally a hand trowel, and frequently, just your hands. If the soil between rows is not regularly chopped and stirred with a hoe, it can form a hard crust that will obstruct the passage of air, water, and nutrients down towards the plants' roots. Weeds grow faster than many kinds of seedlings, and can effectively deprive developing crops of vital supplies of sunlight and nutrients. Weeds also provide convenient shelter for a variety of harmful insects. Sometimes, it will seem a battle you cannot win, but you must try to keep your garden free of weeds. Weeds are survivors, tough and adaptible, but diligent work should suffice to keep them under control. Don't ever use weed killing chemicals in a food garden; such poisons can kill vegetables as well; moreover, drawn into a plant through the roots, such chemicals may prove toxic to your family when they eat the plants. After plants are well established, you can relax your efforts somewhat, for the foliage of your crops will shadow the ground and discourage development of weeds close to them.

Begin weeding as soon as seedlings push above the surface. You can avoid mistaking seedlings for weeds by taking a close look at the stalk you're about to pull. If you don't think it's a weed, leave it in the ground until it assumes a definite shape. Your seeds will have been planted in a relatively straight line, so if any green shoots are more than one or two inches away from that imaginary line, on either side, you can assume they're weeds.

It's easiest to weed several hours after a rain shower, or after you've watered the plot. Wait until the plants have dried out, but try to get out there before the soil has dried entirely. The ground will still be rather soft, and the weeds will come out easily. Give each a gentle tug. The looser the soil, the less likely you are to inadvertently damage the roots or nearby seedlings. Cultivate the ground between rows after you have finished weeding around the plants. Bring the blade of the hoe towards you, pulling it gently through the soil. But remember to keep such cultivation shallow, so as not to damage any plant roots lying close to the surface. By working the soil with a hoe, you not only remove established weeds and keep the soil loose; you expose weed seeds encouraged to germinate by the rain. Air and sunlight will soon dry them out, and this will prove fatal to them. After you finish weeding, gather up the waste and take it out of the garden. Add the weeds to your compost pile, or throw them out, but don't leave weeds lying in your plot. This will only encourage their spread: the pulled stalks can scatter seeds about the rows.

I don't know of any gardener who enjoys weeding. In summer heat it can prove a grim business. But it is absolutely necessary. If you don't keep weeds out of your garden, all of the time and effort you've spent preparing and planting your garden will have been wasted. Weed your garden. Weed it thoroughly. And weed it frequently.

Water

Plants cannot survive long without water. It is the medium through which vital nutrients are drawn in through the plants' roots, as well as an essential factor in many other plant processes. In most areas, rain occurs too irregularly to supply all of the moisture vegetable plants need. So you will have to supplement the rainfall by watering the garden.

How frequently you will have to water depends on the weather. For proper growth and large yields, your plants will need at least an inch of rain a week. You can purchase a rain gauge at a garden center or from several mail supply houses, to keep track of the amount of rain that has fallen. Or you can place several tin cans in various parts of your garden. Draw lines on the inner walls of the can, at intervals of an inch. After a rain, check them — or your rain gauge — to find out how much rain fell on the garden. Keep a record of the amount and the date. If less than an inch fell, and if there are no more showers within the next three or four days, it will then be time to water again. During very warm, sunny weather, you will have to water more frequently, since the needs of the plants will increase with the temperature.

The frequency of your watering also depends on the kind of soil in your garden. Sandy soils readily accept water, but do not retain it for any length of time. Soils with a concentration of clay tend to retain water for a much longer time, and should thus be watered less frequently.

There are a variety of watering methods. If you have a very small garden, you can get by with a watering can. Since vegetable plants should be watered thoroughly, however, you will have to make frequent trips to the faucet to do the job properly. If you use a can, shape a saucer-like ridge around the base of each plant, and pour the water into the depression. This will allow the water to sink into the soil, instead of merely flowing away from the plant. Don't pour water onto the foliage; water enters a plant through its roots, not its leaves. Moreover, beads of moisture on leaves can act as miniature magnifying glasses, focusing and intensifying the sunlight and causing burns to appear under the beads.

Most gardeners water their plots with a hose. Your hose should have a nozzle adjusted to provide a fine spray. You can prop the hose up with a forked stick or a rock, placing the hose at the end of the walkway between two rows. Move it to another walkway after twenty minutes. In this way, you can avoid standing in the hot sun for lengthy periods. Perforated plastic hoses, which are available at garden supply centers and hardware stores, are well suited for use in a vegetable garden. Lay the hose between two rows. When the water is sent through the hose, moisture is sent out as a fine spray, falling on either side of the hose.

If you live in an area where there is little appreciable rainfall, you can dig furrows (actually miniature irrigation ditches) between rows. The furrows should be dug before you plant and should be at least a foot wide, with sloped sides, and about six inches deep. Each furrow should be no more than five inches away from a row. To provide water for thirsty crops, fill the furrows almost to the top with water. The water will gradually soak into the soil towards the crops' roots.

Sprinklers are often mentioned as a convenient watering method. But they have some drawbacks. A sizable amount of the water they throw out never reaches the soil. It evaporates, or else lands on foliage, where it is useless. Moreover, because a sprinkler takes more time to water a garden thoroughly, it will increase your water bill. I don't think it's efficient enough to use by itself, though it may prove worthwhile as an occasional supplement to your watering practices.

When you water, water thoroughly and slowly. Moisture should seep into the soil. A forceful stream of water will simply run along the surface, and carry along with it valuable nutrients and soil. Water in the morning, since during the day is when plants need water and nutrients. Never water in the evening — your plants don't need the moisture then, and it may prove harmful by providing a medium for the growth of molds and mildews.

Unless the weather has been exceptionally hot and dry, one thorough watering a week should be sufficient. Specifically, your garden will need at least an inch of water a week.

Before you water, use a hoe to stir up the soil. Watering can turn soil that has already hardened into an impermeable crust — so keep your soil loose.

Fertilizer

Strictly speaking, fertilizer is not plant "food." Plants don't eat nutrients. Instead, they use some seventeen different elements, in combination with sunlight, to manufacture their own food. Nutrients are just the raw elements for that process. The point, however, is that if plants can't draw sufficient nutrients in through their roots, they can't produce the food they need to fuel the growth of roots, foliage, and fruit. All parts of a plant become stunted and sickly if denied food. Eventually, the plant will die. Of course, many of the nutrients a plant depends on will be present in your soil, but possibly not in quantities sufficient to satisfy the plant's needs. So you must supplement the supply by adding fertilizer and organic materials to your garden.

Nitrogen, phosphorus, and potassium are the elements most important for plant health and growth. Nitrogen stimulates the rapid growth of stems and leaves. Phosphorus encourages root formation. Potassium makes plants better able to resist disease, and it also encourages steady growth, as well as the ability to produce fruit. A "complete" fertilizer offers all three of these elements in a balanced mix. Inspect the label on a bag of fertilizer, and you'll find three numbers printed under the brand name. These numbers, such as 5-10-5, 4-8-4, or 6-12-6, indicate the percentage of each in the mix. Nitrogen is always indicated by the first number, phosphorus by the second, potassium by the third. The order never changes. Thus 4-8-4 would mean that four percent of the mix is composed of nitrogen, eight percent is phosphorus, and five percent potassium. The rest of the mix is composed of inert materials (such as sterilized soil) and small amounts of the other fourteen necessary elements.

To determine how many pounds of a nutrient a mix contains, multiply the total weight of the bag by the number representing that element in the mix. So a one hundred pound bag of 4-8-4 fertilizer will contain four pounds of nitrogen, eight of phosphorus, and four of potassium. That may not sound like very much, but the elements are present in a highly concentrated form. A little of such a mix should go a long way.

How often you apply fertilizer depends greatly upon the kind of soil in your garden, as well as on the crops you are growing. A light, sandy soil will not retain nutrients for any length of time, and may require as many as four dressings during the summer. A heavier soil, one having a high percentage of clay, retains both nutrients and water for a longer period of time, and should need only two applications of fertilizer. Generally, it is better to apply several small applications of a fertilizer, rather than a single dressing. What your plants need is a steady supply, not just one terrific dose.

How much fertilizer should you use? The rule-of-thumb most often mentioned is five to six pounds of a complete fertilizer for every one hundred row feet. This is a guideline, however, not a commandment engraved on stone. You may need more or less, depending on how healthy your soil is.

Before you sow any seeds, or move seedlings outdoors, you should apply a liberal amount of a complete fertilizer to the garden, and use a rake to mix it in thoroughly with the first three inches of soil. Turn and mix the soil and fertilizer until there are no large clumps of either to be found. Do this during the week when you intend to do your planting.

On the day you plan to sow the garden, mark out each row with a length of string stretched between two blocks of wood. This will help you to keep the rows straight, and will indicate where to apply a dressing of fertilizer. After the rows are laid out, dig furrows three inches deep on either side of each. The furrows should be three to four inches away from a row. Spread a complete fertilizer in the furrows, to a depth of from one to one-and-a-half inches. Then cover the furrows with a layer of soil, until the surface of the garden is once again level. Now you can plant the seeds.

If you are transplanting seedlings begun indoors, you can give them a dose of fertilizer when they are set in the ground. Because seedlings are already well advanced, they need nutrients immediately — and they need more than seeds do. Dissolve a 5-10-5 fertilizer in water, at the ratio of one pound of mix to five gallons of water. Stir until most of the fertilizer has dissolved. Place a seedling in its hole, fill the hollow half way with soil, then pour in a cupful of the mix. Brush in the remainder of the soil. The liquid makes nutrients available to them as soon as they have been transplanted.

Several weeks after the seeds and seedlings have been planted, dress the garden with another load of fertilizer. Spread a mix along both sides of each row, being careful to make sure that no fertilizer actually touches the plants. It's strong stuff, and can burn a seedling's tender tissue. The mix should be laid over the soil, six to eight inches from a row. Apply it at a rate of from two to five pounds for every hundred row feet, depending on the number of times you've already applied fertilizer, and on the consistency and condition of your soil. (See chapter 5 for an explanation of soil types, soil testing, and methods for improving the soil.)

You'll find a remarkable variety of fertilizers at garden supply centers. The label on a bag will list its components, the percentage of each in the mix, and will also explain how it should be applied. Complete fertilizers are composed of manufactured elements. Organic fertilizers, which have become increasingly popular in recent years, are composed of materials occuring naturally — e.g., humus — or produced as a byproduct of a living substance — e.g., manure. Common organic sources of nutrients include:

Nitrogen — bone meal, blood meal, cottonseed meal, fish meal emulsion, and animal manures;

Phosphorus — bone meal, phosphate rock;

Potassium — potash rock, seaweed, wood ashes.

88

Chemical fertilizers are concentrated, so a smaller amount will go a long way; that makes them less expensive. Organic fertilizers are generally sold separately, and are applied individually to the garden. They are not concentrated, and so may prove somewhat more expensive than chemicals. But they take a longer time to dissolve, and as a result, don't have to be applied as frequently.

More importantly, recent research (see Bibliography for a list of sources) indicates that the exclusive use of chemical fertilizers depletes and damages the soil. The soil in your garden is a delicately balanced ecosystem, of such complexity that all of its processes have yet to be identified. The structure of the soil — that is, its ability to admit, retain, and release air, water, and nutrients — requires the presence of a variety of organic materials. These materials are present in organic fertilizers, in compost, and even in mulches, but not in chemical mixes. By treating the soil with nothing but chemicals, this delicate ecosystem of the soil can be disrupted, and the structure of the soil damaged. A soil out of balance is vulnerable to infections, since bacteria that have been controlling disease organisms are no longer present in sufficient quantities to do the job. Many nutrients cease to be produced in the soil, and greater and greater quantities of chemicals are required to keep plants going.

This is a controversial subject, and the argument has yet to be finally resolved, but this much can be said: it makes good sense to treat your soil in the best way possible. And soil benefits from the addition of organic materials — so give your soil some. Compost is an excellent soil conditioner (see chapter 5) Remember: the better the shape of your soil the fewer chemicals you will have to add to it — and the healthier your plants will be.

You may want to pursue the subject, so I've included a list of articles and books covering the topic in the Bibliography. Until you reach a decision, or until the argument is settled by indisputable research, I suggest you treat your soil, and your crops, with both organic and chemical fertilizers. Try to keep your soil in condition, and supplement organic materials with a chemical mix.

Chapter  Eight

HARVESTING

Most gardeners find themselves at harvest time with more vegetables than their families can immediately consume. Indeed, if you've taken proper care of your garden, it's almost impossible not to have more than you need. A good harvest is the result of careful, patient gardening. But what do you do with the surplus? Well, you can parcel it out to appreciative friends, and you may be able to sell some of it. Better still, by using one of several inexpensive techniques, you can store it, and assure yourself of a supply of fresh vegetables throughout the fall and into the winter.

Vegetables can remain fresh for practically any length of time, provided they are kept away from light, in an environment having a low temperature, a regular supply of moisture, and adequate ventilation. If you have a basement, you can build a storage room in an unused corner. If you don't have a cellar, or if you don't want anything quite so elaborate, store your surplus in a coldframe, in a barrel buried in the ground, in a pit, or even in cardboard boxes filled with sawdust.

If a steady, year-long supply of vegetables is a primary reason you've started a garden, you will need a spacious storage area. If you have a cellar, you should consider building a storage room. The best location in your cellar would be the north-east corner, where it will remain slightly cooler than elsewhere. The room should, of course, be located as far away as possible from your furnace or heating system. Use two-by-fours and plywood to construct the two outside walls. You'll need a sound door, fitted tightly to the frame. The exterior walls and the ceiling of the unit should be insulated with three-and-a-half inch fiberglass. If your basement is continuously damp, as indeed most basements are, build the room in the corner having a window. While you will have to cover the glass with a thick sheet of cardboard to reduce the light level in the unit, having it in the unit will give you a source of ventilation that can be used to reduce dampness. Open the window when the basement feels very damp. A hygrometer is an inexpensive instrument that registers the amount of humidity in the air. A psychrometer indicates both the temperature and the level of humidity in a room. Either would prove a helpful addition to your unit. When the level of humidity climbs above sixty percent, you will have to provide some additional ventilation to dissipate the humid dampness. If you can't build the unit around a window, you will have to set a vent into one wall.

A room temperature ranging from thirty-two to fifty-five degrees will be suitable for preserving most vegetables. Different areas in the room will have differing temperatures. Indeed, the temperature variation within a storage room may be as much as ten degrees. This still permits storing various vegetables in the environment best suited for them. For instance, the closer one gets to the ceiling, the higher the temperature will be, because heat always rises. Onions don't store well in very cold conditions, so they should be hung near the ceiling. Root crops remain their freshest when kept in very cool conditions, so they should be stored close to the ground. Squash prefers an intermediate temperature, in the middle forties, and should be stored on shelves or racks halfway up the wall. If you don't have a cellar, or if you judge your harvest too small for such an elaborate arrangement, you can store excess root crops in a pit, barrel or cold frame outdoors. Crops can be stored in a pit only in areas in which the temperature rarely falls far below freezing.

You can construct a pit for crop storage by excavating a wide hole two and a half feet deep. Line the pit with leaves or straw, and pile the crops in cone-shaped stacks. A layer of straw should separate crops. Cover the pit with a final thick layer of straw, and spade six inches of soil over the straw. Use plenty of straw, for soil should not be allowed to touch the crops.

A large barrel makes an excellent inexpensive root cellar. Large, sturdy barrels are available at some hardware stores and lumber yards. Many department stores receive merchandise packed in barrels, and you may be able to secure several barrels from such a source. Dig a hole in the ground slightly larger than the barrel, so that it can be laid in the ground at a forty-five degree angle. Before dropping the barrel into place, arrange several large stones or bricks at the bottom of the hole, to improve drainage. Wash the barrel out before you use it. Check its interior for any splinters or projecting nails. Remove any that you find. Move the barrel into place, and spade soil into the hole around the barrel until it is firmly in place. Line the barrel with straw, and pack it with alternating layers of root vegetables and straw. When it has been filled, fit the lid on and pile a thick layer of leaves, straw or mulch over and around that part of the barrel projecting above ground. A board or large rock, positioned over the mound, will further protect the contents of the barrel from the prying paws of small mammals.

A coldframe can be converted into a root cellar by packing it with alternate layers of straw and root crops. The layer on the bottom should be of straw, as should the layer on the top. You can then cover the entire unit with a mulch, or with a sheet of canvas, to protect the vegetables from sunlight.

The size and complexity of your storage unit depends on how much you have to store, and how much you can afford to spend. If you're considering building a unit, remember that only root crops can be stored in a barrel, pit or coldframe. All kinds of vegetables can be stored in a basement unit. Whatever design you select, you will have to have the unit ready by the time the crops are to be harvested. Once you harvest a crop, it cannot be left lying about. You'll have to be ready to do something with it. So plan ahead.

If you decide to store part of your harvest, set only the best looking vegetables aside. Top quality vegetables keep best: blemished produce is likely to rot or become infected. If you do store some "less-than-perfect" vegetables, keep them separate from the others, and use them first. If you discover rotting, bruised or infected vegetables in your storage area or container, discard them immediately.

Handle all of your vegetables carefully, but be especially careful with vegetables marked for storage. Make certain that they aren't bruised or scratched. The interior of a container should be smooth, and free of sharp surfaces. The walls of your storage room should be cleared of projecting nails or other pointed materials, for your safety as well as the safety of your crops. Never store vegetables directly on soil, or on the floor of a storage area. Vegetables need air circulating all around them to remain fresh. The part of a vegetable pressed to the ground, and thus cut off from the air, will become moist and begin to rot. Don't store any vegetable, except tomatoes, until it has ripened. Green tomatoes can be wrapped in newspaper and stored indoors, where they will ripen.

Crops selected for storage should be removed from a plant with several inches of stem still attached. Root crops should be pulled and allowed to lay in the sun for several hours before being stored: sunlight will kill the roots, causing the vegetable to cease growing. Carefully brush soil off of vegetables, but don't wash them. Washing a vegetable causes it to store poorly.

It isn't difficult to store a crop, and it needn't be an expensive or elaborate undertaking. Storing crops will certainly lower your food bills, as you continue to enjoy fresh home grown vegetables through the fall and into the winter.

PESTS & DISEASES

If you have a garden, you're certain to have bugs in it. That shouldn't, however, be a cause for alarm. Many of the bugs will just be passing through, on their way to other, more attractive environments. Some will take up permanent residence in and around your garden, but will have no interest in your crops. A few species of insects will be attracted to your garden as a likely source of nourishment — but that doesn't mean you have to wheel out the heavy artillery every time you spot what you think is a dangerous pest. I urge you to resist the impulse to reach for a poison each time you discover a ragged leaf or a suspicious bug. Most pest attacks can be controlled with non-chemical techniques. If chemicals are required, there are several poisons available that are strong enough to do the job, but pose no threat to warm blooded creatures, such as your dog, your cat, or you.

You can avoid some pest attacks by keeping your garden free of weeds and other debris — such material can both attract, and hide, pests. Healthy plants are said to be less vulnerable to attack than undernourished plants. While this idea is by no means proven, it does make good sense to give your plants the moisture and nutrients they need. If a reduction in pests attacks is a result of raising healthy crops, all the better.

Some herbs and ornamental plants repel insects. By creating a border of such plants around your most vulnerable crops, or by scattering the seeds of such plants at intervals along crop rows, you can discourage some insect attacks. For instance, garlic, scattered among rows of lettuce and peas, drives away aphids. Leeks, planted among carrots, discourage the attention of carrot flies. Radishes, mixed among rows of cucumbers, repel cucumber beetles. Radishes are also used by some gardeners as a decoy. Planted alongside a row of a leaf vegetable, they draw away leaf-eating pests that would otherwise damage the more valuable crop. Tansy planted around or among cabbage plants will protect the crop from all but the most determined cabbage worms. Tansy is also said to have a noticeable deterrent effect on cutworms and some species of beetles. Marigolds planted around a potato patch help keep Colorado potato beetles at bay. The plant also has a mysterious effect on nematodes, microscopic worms that attack the roots of crops, serving to drive them off. Placing these plants around and among your vegetables won't eliminate pests from your garden, but sufficient evidence is available to prove that these herbs and plants do have a noticeable deterrent effect.

You should also consider using an insect to control an insect. Some species of insect's survive by preying on other bugs. Ladybugs, familiar visitors to most gardens, have voracious appetites and a special fondness for aphids, one of the most troublesome garden pests. If you'd like to encourage ladybug activity in your garden, you can purchase a supply of the bug at some garden supply centers, or through the mail (see Resources for a list of suppliers). Companies selling ladybugs frequently advertise in gardening magazines.

The Praying Mantis is probably the best insect friend your garden could have. This thin, dainty relative of the grasshopper lives on a diet composed entirely of garden pests. While the mantis averages only four inches in length, it has a startlingly persistent appetite. Given an insect rich environment, mantids will go on eating all day. You can purchase egg bundles of mantids through the mail. The bundles should be tied to a shrub or a limb of a small bush. When the eggs hatch, the young will disperse throughout the garden. Unless you have a very large garden, or woods close at hand, you won't need many mantids. Fifty to one hundred eggs will be all you need for most gardens.

The dark brown or black ground beetle has a shield-shaped body. It conceals itself in the soil during the day, emerging at night to hunt down a meal of worms, snails and caterpillars.

The Aphis or Ant Lion is the larvae of a winged insect. They feed on the eggs of many types of caterpillars, and on full grown mites, aphids and mealybugs.

Dragonflies, and their smaller, more delicate relative the Damselfly, live around ponds, lakes and marshes. While they feed primarily on mosquitoes, they also eat many kinds of soft bodied insects. If they appear in your garden, don't disturb them. They're probably looking for food, and the more meals they make of pests in your vegetable patch, the less you'll have to worry about.

There are many more predators of insects, including wasps, spiders, toads and some species of birds. While their preferences in pests may vary widely, they do have one thing in common. Pesticides applied to a garden to destroy pests will have an almost equally destructive effect on predators. Poison is an indiscriminate weapon — it kills both friend and foe. Unfortunately, many predator populations recover much more slowly from pesticides than pest populations. The pests, being more prolific, may quickly recover from an application of poison. Because there are fewer predators to control the new generation of pests, you may actually increase your problems by waging chemical warfare in your garden. Pesticides should be your last line of defense.

Aluminum foil has recently been proved to be a remarkably effective ally in the gardener's war on pests. The foil repels aphids, one of the most serious and stubborn of garden pests, because it confuses their sense of direction. Yellow attracts aphids. Indeed, they seem to search out the color, knowing instinctively that it indicates an edible plant. The foil reflects streaks of blue sky — and aphids always steer clear of the color. Aluminum foil also, for some reason yet unknown, encourages the activity of some predators, and draws honeybees to a garden. Because the bees are a source of pollination, they should be a welcome presence in any vegetable patch.

Lay strips of foil over the rows in your garden. Punch holes in the material to accommodate the seedlings. Press the foil gently down over them, so that it rests lightly on the surface of the ground. In tests, crops of broccoli, cabbage, cucumbers and squash all were free of aphids throughout their growth when mulched with foil.

Black light traps can be used to lure many kinds of flying insects active during the hours of darkness. Anywhere from a pint to a quart of insects can be lured to and destroyed by a light trap each night. Because most insect predators, and other beneficial insects such as wasps and bees, are active only during the day, a light trap can be used without upsetting the balance of power in your garden.

Many pests are large enough to be hand-picked off plants. If you can see a pest at work, it's large enough for you to lift off and destroy. If you can't reach them, or if you'd prefer not to, or if the individual pests are too small for you to get a grip on them, a strong stream of cool water directed onto the leaves of an infested plant will discourage most insects.

Companion planting, the introduction of insect predators and other simple methods of control may not be enough to rid your plot of pests. But such techniques can certainly reduce pest populations to such a point that only very mild pesticides need be used.

There are a variety of insecticides made from plant derivatives. They are certainly the safest of all the poisons. Pyrethum is a poison made from the dried flowers of a species of chrysanthemum. It is said to pose no threat to warm blooded creatures, unless it is consumed in large quantities. Available as an aerosol, it is effective in controlling aphids, caterpillars, leafhoppers and spider mites. Rotenone is derived from chemicals found in the roots of two tropical plants. It is a versatile insecticide, and can be used against aphids, caterpillars, cabbage worms, thrips and other garden pests. Ryania is made from the stem and root of a tropical plant. Available as a powder, it can be used as a dust or mixed with water to make a spray. Aphids, squash bugs and leafhoppers can be eliminated with several applications of the poison.

You can use vegetables to protect vegetables. Onions and hot peppers, ground in a blender along with water to make a thick mush, are said to repel insects when the mix is sprayed onto plant leaves. Strain the mush through a sheet of cheesecloth, and dilute it with enough water to make it sprayable. A teaspoonful of soap or detergent will give the spray greater adhesion. Pour it into a hand sprayer, and apply it to your crops. An application every three days for several weeks should give your crops considerable protection, as many pests will find the mix repellent.

If you've tried everything else, and an infestation shows no signs of abating, you will have to turn to something stronger. Diazinon and malathion are the only two chemical pesticides that are, in my opinion, safe to use in a food garden. Diazinon is used to control insects dwelling under the ground or on its surface, such as cutworms, the larvae of some pests, and sowbugs. It is generally dissolved in water and applied as a drench to the soil. Malathion can be used against most pests, but it seems to be especially effective in the control of aphids, mealybugs, spider mites and thrips.

When you use a poison, follow the directions given for its application to the letter. And don't use it more frequently than the directions indicate.

I don't use chemical insecticides, because I believe that they cause much more harm than they are worth. Sufficient evidence now exists to strongly suggest that insecticides have many harmful side effects, frequently causing a severe disruption of the ecosystem. However, I have no intention of pushing my convictions on you. I do urge you to read some of the literature now available on the subject before you begin using chemical insecticides. I think you will find the evidence sobering enough to make you reconsider using chemicals in your garden. The decision is entirely your own.

If you keep your garden clean, watch it closely for any signs of an invasion, and use a variety of methods to discourage pests, you will escape many serious problems. You are bound to lose some plants to pests — but so long as those losses are small and infrequent, there is no cause for alarm. Insects are a natural component of your garden. Learn to treat them as such, learn how to control them, and you need never become involved in chemical warfare.

Pests

While many species of insects are potential troublemakers, only about a dozen species show up with any frequency. Pests capable of causing serious damage include:

Aphids. The most numerous and troublesome of all the garden pests. Aphids attach themselves to the undersides of leaves and suck juices from the plant. A prolonged attack causes plants to pale, become weak and stunted, and to cease producing fruit. Aphids are so small that only a close inspection of an ailing plant will disclose their presence. Lady bugs and some species of wasps are the most efficient natural method for controlling an aphid attack. A strong stream of water directed onto a plant will knock many, but not necessarily all, of the aphids off. Rotenone or pyrethrum can also be used to halt an infestation.

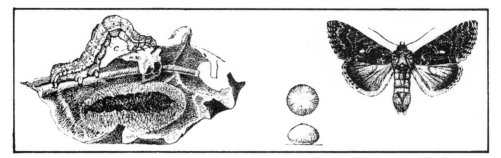

Cabbage loopers. Loopers are known in some areas as **measuring worms**, because of their method of locomotion. These worms double themselves up in a pronounced loop as they crawl. Loopers feed on cabbage in all stages of growth. Malathion is the best control. If only a few loopers are present, they can be removed by hand.

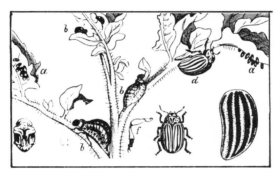

Colorado potato beetle. This yellow and black striped bug can cause serious damage to crops of eggplant, peppers, potatoes and tomato seedlings. The bugs are large enough to be hand picked off. Search the undersides of leaves on damaged plants for yellow egg masses. Remove and destroy any leaves having egg cases attached.

Corn earworm. The earworm is a green or brown pest that feeds on corn silk, interferring with pollination, or works its way into a cob, where it feasts on the kernels. After corn has pollinated, use an eyedropper to apply mineral oil to the silks.

Cucumber beetle. The eastern species of this pest has a striped body. The western form is spotted. The beetles attack beans, cucumbers, peas and squash.

Because they favor seedlings, keep a close watch on these crops for the first month after sowing. The bugs are large enough to be removed by hand. Spraying young plants with rotenone or malathion will discourage the pest.

Cutworms. These caterpillars emerge at night to feed on the tender tissue of young plant stems. Placing collars around seedlings will prevent attacks. If the cutworms seem a persistent problem in your garden, you may have to search them out by night, and remove and destroy any that you locate.

Leaf miners. This pest burrows into leaves, feeding on the tissue within. Its feeding creates tunnels that are quite noticeable. Pepper and spinach seem to be especially attractive to leaf miners. Remove any damaged leaves, and treat infested plants with Diazinon.

Mexican bean beetle. Bean beetles are copper colored, and have a fondness for any kind of beans. The beetle larvae cluster on the undersides of leaves. Hand pick the adults. Clip off leaves supporting larvae. Rotenone can be sprayed on affected plants to prevent a reoccurence of the beetle.

Slugs and snails. Although neither the slug nor the snail are insects, they can hold their own in any competition of garden pests. They feed on a wide variety of plants, tearing great chunks out of foliage. A mulch of oak leaves repels both pests. Sawdust, sand or ashes scattered around plants discourages the tender bodied slug. Both pests can be hand picked. Traps are available, but should not be necessary in most gardens. Shallow saucers of beer, pushed into the ground near plants at dusk, will attract these pests. Either before or after sampling the brew, they will fall into the saucers and drown.

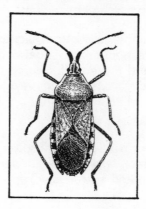

Squash bug. This brown bug lives by sucking the juice from the leaves of squash plants. The leaves will noticeably wilt. Handpick the adults. Remove and destroy any leaves having red egg clusters attached to their undersides.

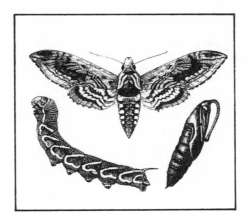

Tomato hornworms. These large worms are certainly distinctive in appearence. They feed on the leaves of tomato plants and, less frequently, on eggplant and pepper leaves. All you need do is lift the pests off and destroy them.

Thrips. Thrips are small winged insects. They feed on leaves, causing them to develop blotches, to turn brown and to fall off. Malathion is the most effective control.

White fly. The white fly is a tiny pest that gathers on the undersides of leaves. You may not suspect their presence until you accidentally brush a leaf, causing a white cloud to spring into the air and circle the plant. Tomatoes and eggplants are frequent hosts. Malathion can help to control an infestation. If you purchase seedlings of either tomatoes or eggplants, buy only from a dealer that you, or someone you know, has dealt with before, as white flies are frequently a problem in greenhouses, where seedlings are raised.

Plant Diseases

Plant diseases are unlikely to pose much of a threat to your crops, if you keep the ground free of debris and provide adequate supplies of moisture and nutrients for the plants. Healthy plants resist disease. Plants weakened by inadequate or improper care are especially vulnerable to infection.

If a disease does strike, it is generally easier to contain than an insect invasion, for each disease has differing host plants. It would be impossible for a disease to sweep through your entire garden. Usually, a disease affects only one or two crops, while the rest of the garden remains untouched and healthy. Among the affected crops, only some of the plants will show symptoms of illness, while others will continue growing normally.

You can often save a plant damaged by insects. But if a plant has been infected, the best thing to do is pull it out and discard it immediately. Don't add diseased plants to your compost pile, for there is a good chance many disease spores will survive the warmth generated within the pile, and thus have a second chance to infect plants, when the compost is applied.

The best way to deal with plant diseases in your patch is to prevent their occurence. It's important that you treat your soil with fertilizer, compost and other amendments, to make it friable and rich in nutrients. The more nutrients your crops have to draw on, the healthier they will be.

Many seed companies now offer seeds developed to be disease resistant. While treated seeds are more expensive than untreated seeds of the same crop, the greatly reduced likelihood of an infection occuring makes them well worth the cost. When you buy seedlings, examine them closely for any signs of disease, such as mottled leaves, weak stems or deformed roots.

Keep your garden free of debris. Weed it frequently. If some plants do become infected, clean any tools you use to handle the plants before using them again in the garden. Don't smoke when you're in the garden. The tobacco mosaic virus, which attacks such crops as eggplant, peppers and tomatoes, can be spread through a garden by the smoke from your cigarette or pipe.

Don't neglect your garden. Check it daily, and if you think a crop needs water or a dressing of fertilizer, don't put off giving it what it needs. Keep a close eye on your plants. If a crop shows signs of trouble, investigate immediately. If you can't identify the symptoms, take a sample afflicted plant to your agricultural agent or state extension service. And don't panic — disease attacks are infrequent, and can be quickly contained when they occur.

Diseases are caused by viruses, bacteria, or fungus spores. Virus diseases are spread by insects, including mites, nematodes and, frequently, aphids. The symptoms of a virus infection include pale splotches on leaf surfaces, stunted growth and leaves that have become dry and misshapen.

Bacteria enter a plant through its pores, or through a cut made in the stem or roots of a plant by a carelessly used tool. Plants suffering from a bacterial infection develop soft spots, patches of rotting tissue.

Fungus diseases are caused by spores, which attach themselves to plants to obtain food. Black, brown or yellow spots on leaves, or a powdery coating on leaves indicate the presence of a fungus.

Specific diseases occuring in vegetables include:

Anthracnose. It's presence is indicated by black or reddish brown sunken spots on leaves or stems. Leaves eventually wither and drop off. Beans, cucumbers, peppers and tomatoes are all vulnerable to the fungus. Use a fungicide such as maneb or zineb to protect healthy plants. Pull out and immediately discard any plants showing definite signs of infection.

Blossom End Rot. End rot causes the skin of peppers, squash and tomatoes dry and brittle. Sunken spots either very pale or brown-black blemish the fruit. Inadequate watering, or erratic watering practices encourage its development. During periods of dry, hot weather keep the soil evenly moist. A shallow layer of mulch will help maintain an even soil temperature. Discard damaged fruit.

Early and late Blights. Irregular dark brown or black spots appear on leaves and stems during an attack of early blight. Leathery dark spots appear on the bottom of fruit. The symptoms of late blight include greenish-black wet spots, and a thin white mold on the underside of leaves. The blights affect only potatoes and tomatoes, and can be prevented by growing these crops in well-drained soil. Maneb can be used to save plants showing the first symptoms of infection. Rotate these crops each year — and never plant one where the other has been in the previous season.

Mildews. Downy mildew is indicated when the leaves of beans and cucumbers develop yellow, brown or black areas. A powdery white mold can be found on the underside of leaves, and on bean pods. Powdery mildew causes a white or brown growth, rather gritty to the touch, to appear on the leaves and stems of squash, cucumbers and beans. Fruit will wither, plants cease growing and die. Maneb can be used on beans and cucumbers, to control a mildew that is not greatly advanced. Karathane can be used to treat squash plants, if the mildew is discovered while in an early stage. Rotate these plants, never sowing one crop in a space vacated by either of the others.

Rots. A variety of rots occur in vegetable plants, affecting various parts of a plant. Rots cause plant or fruit tissue to become soft and pulpy. Plants become yellow and stunted, as they become incapable of absorbing nutrients. Eventually, they die. Constantly wet soil makes an excellent environment for the growth of rots bacteria. Don't overwater your garden. You can improve the consistency of soil having inadequate drainage by mixing soil amendments into it. Pull out and immediately discard affected plants.

Rust. This fungus is fatal to asparagus. Yellowish-orange boils on leaves and stems indicate an attack of rust. Cut affected plants at ground level and get rid of them immediately. Use rust-resistant asparagus seeds. Sow the crop elsewhere, if you plant more the following year.

A fungicide is a chemical preparation that can be used to treat diseased plants and protect healthy crops from infection. Fungicides are available as either wettable powders or dusts. Dusts, as the name implies, are dusted onto affected plant parts. Powders must be dissolved in water, and can be sprayed on plants, or poured onto the soil around infected plants, to destroy soil borne diseases. Captan, Ferbam, Maneb and Zineb are all fungicides.

Gardening with Children

If the daily chores of tending a vegetable patch are getting you down, I can't think of a better way to liven up your garden than to invite your children into it. Kids can do most of the things you can do in the plot, if they're shown how. In fact, I have known several families where the children were the most enthusiastic and capable gardeners.

Gardening seems to me to be an almost ideal family project. It's something the entire family can do. It's inexpensive. It's an excellent form of modest exercise. And it provides an opportunity for you to introduce your children to the intricate marvels of the natural world.

Gardening can encourage a child to develop patience; and a sense of responsibility. More importantly, it offers almost limitless educational possibilities. Kids will have a chance to view, and participate in, the process of natural growth and development. If you encourage your children to follow their vegetables into the kitchen, they can learn something about the preparation of food and the basics of cooking. Because many facets of gardening involve measurements, working in the family garden gives kids a chance to practice their arithmetic. Your children might want to investigate the history of farming. Remember too that you can do a good deal more with vegetables than just eat them. There are any number of things you can make with vegetables. For children growing up in an urban area, a small garden offers them an intimate link with a natural world elsewhere hidden by concrete and tarmac. Most importantly, when you bring your children into the garden, you give them a chance to feel deep satisfaction and pride in something they have done, by themselves.

Gardening shouldn't be a grim business. If you've forgotten that, it's time you learned a lesson from your children.

The Ortho Division of the Chevron Chemical Company publishes an excellent pamphlet on kids and gardening. Titled "A Child's Garden, A Guide for Parents and Teachers", you can get a free sample copy by writing

Public Relations — ORTHO
200 Bush Street
San Francisco, California 94120

RESOURCES

Carts

Garden Way Research
Charlotte, Vermont
05445

Offer three cart models, shipped as kits or fully assembled. Free literature is available on request.

Vermont-Ware
Department 704
Hinesburg, Vermont
05461

Two models available. Free literature sent on request.

Insect Control

Sources of Beneficial Insects

Bio-Control Company
10180 Ladybird Drive
Auburn, California 95603

Ladybugs

California Green Lacewings
2410 J Street
Merced, California
95340

Lacewings
Trichogramma fly

Eastern Biological Control Company Route 5, Box 379 Jackson, New Jersey 08527	Praying mantid egg cases
Organic Supply Company P.O. Box 1607 444 Lincoln Way Auburn, California 95603	Ladybugs, Praying mantid egg cases
West Coast Ladybug Sales P.O. Box 242 Biggs, California 95917	

Magazines

Countryside Magazine Countryside & Small Stock Rt. 1 Box X Waterloo, Wisconsin 53594	12 issues a year for $9.00. Articles on raising stock, gardening etc.
Mother Earth News P.O. Box 70 Hendersonville, North Carolina 28739	Write for subscription rates.
Organic Gardening & Farming 33 East Minor Street Emmaus, Pennsylvania 18049	12 issues a year for $6.85.

Manufacturers of Organic Fertilizers

Some of these products, or similar products, should be available at your garden center or from a sales representative offering the products both wholesale and retail. Check your local supplies first. If you can't find what you need, many manufacturers carry on a direct mail order service.

When you write for information and prices, be sure to include a stamped self-addressed envelope. Among the manufacturers and suppliers of organic fertilizers are:

Green Era of Georgia
Route 3, Box 276
Ringgold, Georgia 30736

Joe S. Francis
Blenders, Inc.
Lithonia, Georgia 30058

Maxicrop USA, Inc.   Liquefied Seaweed.
P.O. Box 964   Quart bottle makes
Arlington Heights,   100 gallons.
Illinois 60006

Mer-Made
Box 411
Beverly, Massachusetts 01915

Natural Development   25¢ for a catalog
Company   listing seeds and
Box 215   organic fertilizers.
Bainbridge,
Pennsylvania 17502

New Mexico Humus
P.O. Box 14743
Albuquerque, New Mexico 87111

Odlin Organics
Lakeshore Drive
West Brookfield,
Massachusetts 01585

Plantabbs   Liquid fish fertilizer,
Department 703   available in
Lutherville,   pints, quarts and
Maryland 21093   gallons.
in Canada
Box 329,
Caledonia, Ontario

Sea-Organics Corporation   Organic fertilizer
P.O. Box 127   made with seaweed meal.
Peabody, Maine 01960

Power Tools

Many of the following manufacturers sell through dealers.
Some may also do business through the mail. All of them offer
free information on their tractors and tillers.

Economy Tractor   Free catalog
1005H-4 Anoka Avnue   on Economy tractor
Waukesha, Wisconsin 53186 and its accessories.

FMC Corporation   Line of tillers and
Port Washington,   tractors. For address
Wisconsin 53074   of nearest distributor
                            write the company.

106

Garden-Way Manufacturing Company, Inc. Troy-Bilt Roto-Tiller Power Composters 102nd Street and Ninth Avenue Troy, New York 12180	Rear-end Rotary tillers and composters, 3 models.
Gilson Brothers Company P.O. Box K2 Plymouth, Wisconsin 53073	Nine models of power tillers.
JiCase Outdoor Power Equipment Division Winneconne, Wisconsin 54986	Company tractors.
Merry Manufacturing Company P.O. Box 168-T Marysville, Wa. 98270	Manufacture the "Merry Tiller".
Precision Valley Manufacturing Company Box 1002 Springfield, Vermont 05156	Yellowbird power cultivator.
Roto-Hoe Company Newburg 2, Ohio 44065	Front or rear mounted tillers.
Wheel Horse Lawn and Garden Tractors 515 West Ireland Road South Bend, Indiana 46614	Rotary powered lawn and garden tractors.

Non-chemical Pesticides

Galt Research Inc.
RR 1, Box 245-GI
Trafalgar, Indiana 46181

Manufacture Dipel
a natural bacterium
harmful to leaf-eating
insects, not dangerous
to mammals, earthworms.

Natural Development
Offer Tri-Excel DS,
Box 215
Bainbridge,
Pennsylvania 17502

Company

an insecticide made from
diatomaceous earth, that
is non-toxic to warm
blooded creatures.
25¢ for the catalog.

Nelome's By Organics
915 24th Avenue East
Tuscaloosa, Alabama 35401

Free information on a
line of organic pesticides.

Seedsmen

A World Seed Service
Box 1058
Redwood City,
California 94064

50¢ for the
catalog

Burgess Seed & Plant Company,
P.O. Box 3000
Galesburg, Michigan 49053

Burpee Seeds
300 Park Avenue
Warminster, Pennsylvania 18974

Comstock, Ferre and Company
Wethersfield, Connecticut 06109

D.V. Burrell Seed
Growers Company
Box 150
Rocky Ford, Colorado

Earl May Seed &
Nursery Company
Shenandoah, Iowa 51601

Farmers Seed & Nursery Company
Fairbault, Minnesota 55021

Ferndale Gardens
2360 Nursery Lane
Fairbault, Minnesota 55021

George W. Ball, Inc.
P.O. Box 335
West Chicago, Illinois 60185

George W. Park Seed
Company, Inc.
Greenwood, South Carolina 29647

Gurney Seed & Nursery Company
1448 Page Street
Yankton, South Dakota 57078

Henry Field Seed &
Nursery Company
Shenandoah, Iowa 51602

J.L. Hudson
P.O. Box 1058
Redwood City, California 94604

Joseph Harris Company, Inc.
Moreton Farm
3670 Buffalo Road
Rochester, New York 14624

Kelly Brothers Nurseries
Dansville, New York 14437

Krider Nurseries, Inc.
Box 206A
Middlebury, Indiana 46540

Le Jardin du Gourmet
Ramsey, New Jersey 07446

L.L. Olds Seed Company
2901 Packers Avenue
Box 1069
Madison, Wisconsin 53701

Nichols Garden Nursery   Vegetable catalog 35¢
Pacific North
Albany, Oregon 97321

Natural Development Company
Box 215   25¢ for a catalog of
Bainbridge,   untreated seeds and
Pennsylvania 17502   organic gardening products.

Otis S. Twilley Seed Company
1817 Camden Road
Salisbury, Maryland 21801

Piedmont Plants
Albany, Georgia 31702

Reuter Seed Company, Inc.
New Orleans, Louisiana 70119

Ritchie Feed & Seed Company
27 York Street
Ottawa, Ontario, Canada

Rocky Mountain Seed Company
1325 15th Street
Denver, Colorado 80217

Seedway
P.O. Box 11125
Hall, New York 14463

R.H. Shumway-Seedsman
P.O. Box 777
Rockford, Illinois 61101

Spring Hill Nurseries
110 West Elm Street
Tipp City, Ohio 45371

Stokes Seeds
1965 Stokes Building
Buffalo, New York 14240

Vaughan's Seed Company
Downer s Grove, Illinois 60515

Wetsel Seed Company
Harrisonburg, Virginia 22801

Unless otherwise noted, information from these companies is free. Many start mailing out catalogs as early as January, so get your requests in as early as possible.

Soil Test Kits

Edmund Scientific Company
300 Edscorp Building
Barrington,
New Jersey 08007

Free catalog, test kits from $8.00 up.

Sudbury Laboratory, Inc.
Sudbury,
Massachusetts 01776

Kits from $8.00 up.
Free information.

Pest Control

Birds and small mammals can sometimes badly damage a garden. Some of the non-lethal methods for controlling their feedings are listed below.

Animal Repellents, Inc.
Box 982
Briffin, Georgia 30223

Manufacture the "Bird Barrier"

French Textiles Company
835 Bloomfield Avenue
Clifton, New Jersey 07012

Manufacture "Birds Off" mesh

Havahart
148-B North Water Street
Ossining, New York
10562

Manufacture "Havahart" non-lethal animal traps. 25¢ (credited to the first order) for a booklet and price list.

Ross Daniels Inc.
West Des Moines, Iowa
50265

Garden netting, available in stores, or write manufacturer for information.

Jackson & Perkins Company
1 Rose Lane
Medford, Oregon 97501

BIBLIOGRAPHY

Abraham, George. **Green Thumb Book of Fruit and Vegetable Gardening.** New Jersey: Prentice Hall, 1970. Hardback.

Abraham, Katy. **Raise Vegetables Without a Garden.** Illinois: Countryside Books, 1974. Paperback.
The "Green Thumb" book is a thorough, clear introduction to growing vegetables. "Raise Vegetables Without a Garden" describes the basics of growing vegetables in containers.

Allaby, Michael & Allen, Flyod. **Robots Behind the Plow.** Pennsylvania: Rodale Press, 1974. Hardback.
An indictment of corporate gardening, its methods, and its reliance on chemicals. The "Silent Spring" of gardening books. To get a clear idea of where the vegetables in your supermarket came from, and what's been done to them, read this book.

Alther, Richard & Raymond, Ricard. **Improving Garden Soil with Green Manures.** Vermont: Garden Way Publishing, 1974. Paperback.
The best introduction to the subject of cover cropping.

Brooklyn Botanic Garden. **Handbook on Biological Control of Pests.** New York: Brooklyn Botanic Garden. Paperback.
Complete, rather technical review of controlling pests with other pests. Brooklyn Botanic publishes a series of

excellent handbooks on almost every conceivable
aspect of gardening. Their handbook on vegetable
gardening is quite good.

Bullard, Lacy & Cheek, Art. **Down to Earth Vegetable
Gardening Down South.** 1210 East Park Avenue,
Tallahassee, Florida 32301. Paperback.
A recent, welcome development in publishing are the
regional gardening guides being developed by
independent groups in different regions of the country.
Many of the guides have a pronounced belief in organic
methods.

Campbell, Stu. **The Mulch Book.** Vermont: Garden Way
Publishing, 1973. Paperback.
**Let it Rot! The Home Gardener's Guide to
Composting.** Vermont: Garden Way, 1975.
Stu Campbell's books are clear, compact guides to
complex subjects. His tone is personal, judicious,
confident. I found his books to be the best short guides
to mulching and composting.

Cruso, Thallasa. **Making Vegetables Grow.** New York:
Knopf, 1975. Hardback.
A thorough, personal, readable guide.

Davis, Jeanne ed. **About Community Gardening.**
Everything you need to know about organizing
community gardens. Available from Bridge
Publications, 10632 Little Pautuxent Parkway,
Columbia, Maryland, 21044.

Doty, Walter L., ed. **All About Vegetables.** San Francisco:
Chevron Chemical Company, 1974. Paperback.
Chevron had the clever idea of doing a general book on
vegetable gardening, based on the experiences of both
experts and everyday gardeners, and issuing it in
regional editions. There's an edition for the South,
another for the Northeast, etc. Each edition is basically
similar, differing in having a half-dozen pages devoted to

114

a regions' climates and growing conditions, with specifics on planting dates and temperatures. A good idea, well handled.

Farb, Peter. **Living Earth.** New York: Harper & Row, 1959. Paperback.
A model of good writing, careful research. Not a gardening guide, but an introduction to the composition and functions of soils. Guarranteed to increase your sense of wonder about that collection of materials we so carelessly call "dirt".

Faust, Joan Lee. **The New York Times Book of Vegetable Gardening.** New York: Quadrangle, 1975. Hardback.
A sensible, thorough discussion of the basics. Certainly one of the best of recent vegetable gardening "how-to" books.

Foster, Catherine Osgood. **The Organic Gardener.** New York: Vintage Books, 1972. Paperback.
An excellent guide to the concepts and practises of organic gardening. A warm and convincing introduction to thinking organic.

Gregg, Richard & Philbrick, Helen. **Companion Plants and How to Use Them.** Vermont: Garden Way, Paperback.
I can't imagine anything of consequence having been left out of this book. Exhaustively complete, this is a unique and valuable work.

Hertzberg, Ruth, Vaughan, Beatrice & Greene, Janet. **Putting Food By.** Vermont: Stephen Greene Press. Paperback.
There are several fine books on storing garden harvests. **Putting Food By** is one of the most popular. Clear, specific directions given in a readable style.

Hopp, Henry. **What Every Gardener Should Know About Earthworms.** Vermont: Garden Way, 1973. Paperback.

At last! This pamphlet, by the "world's leading expert on earthworms" debunks the myths concerning earthworms, and explains exactly what they can and cannot do. Certainly the best thing ever written on the subject.

Hylton, William H. **The Rodale Herb Book. How to Use, Grow and Buy Nature's Miracle Plants.**
Pennsylvania: Rodale Press, 1975. Hardback.
Done with the thoroughness and accuracy we've come to expect from Rodale press. Herbs make an excellent border for your vegetable garden. Some even repel insect pests. If you need specific information on an herb, this book should have all you need. Check your library for a copy.

King, F. H. **Farmers of Forty Centuries.** Pennsylvania: Rodale Press. Hardback.
Originally issued in 1911, and now reissued by Rodale, this book is a classic. King toured the Orient at the beginning of the century, with notebook and camera. An expert in agriculture, he recorded the farming techniques then in use in China, Korea and Japan. Composting, mulching and cover cropping were accepted basics in the Orient long before they were practised in the West. I found it an enlightening, and humbling, experience to read how "peasant" cultures were wisely using the principles of organic farming, in a sophisticated form, long before the more "advanced" West. A valuable, even inspiring book.

Kraft, Ken & Kraft, Pat. **Growing Food the Natural Way.**
New York: Doubleday, 1973. Hardback.
Principles and methods of organic gardening, in a clear, detailed text.

Kressy, Michael. **How to Grow Your Own Vegetables.**
New York: Bantam Books, 1975. Paperback.
Complete, readable, well illustrated.

Lerza, Catherine & Jacobson, Michael. **Food for People, Not for Profit.** New York: Ballantine Books, 1975. Why people are starving, and what can be done about it. A well documented book, with specific recommendations for food reforms, both here and abroad.

Loveday, Evelyn. **The Complete Book of Home Storage of Vegetables and Fruits.** Vermont: Garden Way. Paperback.
Thorough instructions, complete, clear illustrations.

Ogden, Samuel. **Step-by-Step to Organic Vegetable Growing.** Pennsylvania: Rodale Press, 1971. Hardback.
Of special interest to gardeners in New England, as Ogden relates his own experiences in adapting his garden to New England soil and climate conditions. A good discussion of gardening techniques, such as soil preparation. Very specific description of planting techniques.

Olkowski, Helga & Olkowski, William. **City People's Book of Raising Food.** Pennsylvania: Rodale Press, 1975. Paperback.
The only book offering specific information on gardening in the city. Complete, clear narrative, inventive techniques.

Philbrick, Helen & Philbrick, John. **The Bug Book.** Vermont: Garden Way Publishing, 1974. Paperback.
Excellent guide to non-chemical methods of dealing with insect pests. This is a book that I've used frequently, and it's information has always paid off.

Raymond, Dick & Cook, Charles. **Down-to-Earth Vegetable Gardening Know-How.** Vermont: Garden Way, 1975. Paperback.
A book on gardening by an experienced gardener. Full

of personal experiences, good gardening tips. Well illustrated. An enjoyable book, and a thorough one.

Rodale, J. I. & Rodale, Robert & Staff. Pennsylvania: Rodale Press.

The Complete Book of Composting, 1960.
Encyclopedia of Organic Gardening, 1959.
The Organic Way to Mulching, 1972.
The Organic Way to Plant Protection, 1966.
Organic Way to Mulching.

Rodale Press has issued some of the best books on organic gardening. The quality of their books is consistently high. Many of the texts are encyclopedic in scope. **Composting** for instance, is a thousand pages long, and seems to cover absolutely everything there is to know about composting. **The Encyclopedia of Organic Gardening** is an invaluable aid to organic gardeners. Thorough, comprehensive, clear texts.

Stomer, John. **The Web of Life.** New York: Signet Books. Paperback.

This wise little book is an excellent introduction to the principles of ecology. The chapters on soil will be of interest to every gardener.

Sunset Books. California: Lane Publishing Company. Paperbacks.

Guide to Organic Gardening, 1973.
Basic Gardening Illustrated, 1974.
Vegetable Gardening, 1975.

Excellent illustrations, clear instructions. Good, brief introductions to gardening.

Tiedjens, Victor. **Encyclopedia of Vegetables.** New York: Barnes & Noble. Paperback.

Packed with information on individual vegetables. Remedies for pest and disease attacks rely too heavily on powerful poisons. Still, a useful book.

Wahlfeldt, Bette. **Gulf Coast Gardening.** General Delivery, Gonzalez, Florida 32560. Paperback.

Guide to growing vegetables in the climatic and soil conditions prevalent in the Gulf coast.

Westcott, Cynthia. **The Gardener's Bug Book.** New York: Doubleday, 1973. Hardback.

A marvelous compendium on all of the insects of potential danger to plants. Good descriptions, explanations of bug behavior, mostly chemical remedies. Although I don't follow many of the remedies, this is a book that I wouldn't want to be without. Check your library for a copy.

Wickenden, Leonard. **Gardening with Nature.** Connecticut: Fawcett Books, 1972. Paperback.

In my opinion, this is the best introduction to the principles and practises of organic gardening. It is clear, complete, and opinionated. I don't always agree with the author, but he presents his positions so fully that I feel I always understand him. This is a long, detailed book, but I think it will amply repay the time you devote to reading it. I find myself rereading passages of it again and again, and learning something new each time.

A list of all the books published on vegetable gardening in the last five years would run for many pages. This bibliography includes only the books that I have read and found to be helpful. You will observe that many of these books have been published by Garden Way or Rodale Press. In the past several years these publishers have issued numbers of books distinguished, in my opinion, by clear, detailed texts and excellent illustrations. While I dislike giving added emphasis to any one publisher, I would be neglecting my responsibility as a writer if I did not indicate the best sources for your further reading. And I do urge you to continue reading about vegetables, for no one book can encompass all there is to know about vegetables. The more you read, the more you are bound to learn — and what you learn can be immediately applied to your garden.

The government is the largest publisher of gardening materials. Most of their pamphlets and books are available for free, or for a comparatively low price. The master list of the publications of the Department of Agriculture is available for 45¢ from the Superintendent of Documents, U.S. Government Printing Office, Washington, D.C. 20404. This master list covers all the publications offered by the U.S.D.A. The U.S.D.A. yearbooks, covering a different topic each year (Soils, Seeds in 1961, Plant Diseases in 1953), are the ultimate sources on their subjects. The state Agricultural Extension Services, located in a state college or university in each of the fifty states, as well as county agricultural agents, keep some publications on hand which they distribute free or for a nominal cost.

In Canada, a free catalog listing low cost and free publications on gardening is available from the Information Division, of Canada's Department of Agriculture, Ottawa, Canada K1A 0C7. Many excellent pamphlets are available from the C.D.A., covering a wide range of subjects.

INDEX